Strengthening the Local Church

A 40 Day Journey to Church Revival

by Roger Hillis

2025: One Stone Press.
All rights reserved. No part of this book may be reproduced
in any form without written permission of the publisher.

Published by:
One Stone Press
979 Lovers Lane
Bowling Green, KY 42103

Printed in the United States of America

ISBN 978-1-966992-12-7

All scripture references, unless otherwise noted, are taken from
the New King James Version, copyright by Thomas H. Nelson, Inc.,
Nashville, Tennessee, 1979, 1980, 1982, 1993.
Used by permission.

1(800)428-0121 • www.onestone.com

Contents

Preface 4
1 – Time to Rebuild 7
2 – Emphasizing the Basics 11
3 – A Deliberate Evangelism Strategy 15
4 – Balanced Preaching 19
5 – New Convert Follow-Up 23
6 – Expecting the Preacher to do Everything 27
7 – Developing a Quality Teaching Program 31
8 – How do You Invite? 35
9 – Effective Gospel Meetings 39
10 – Using Social Media for the Church 43
11 – What if the Church Isn't Growing? 47
12 – Helping Young Men to be Spiritual Leaders 51
13 – A New Evangelistic Idea 55
14 – Major Areas of Church Health 59
15 – How Involved are You? 63
16 – The Core Values 67
17 – The Value of V.B.S. 71
18 – Some Important Leadership Principles 75
19 – The Importance of Worship 79
20 – Improving Our Assemblies 83
21 – Rescue the Perishing 87
22 – Navigating Changes 91
23 – Racially Integrated Churches 95
24 – Effective Teacher Training 99
25 – Leadership: Relationships and Influence 103
26 – Appointing Elders and Deacons 107
27 – Merging for Greater Effectiveness 111
28 – Leading Public Prayer 115
29 – Paying the Price for World Evangelism 119
30 – Generous Giving 123
31 – Standing in the Gap 127
32 – The Importance of Unity 131
33 – The Church in the Twenty-First Century 135
34 – Planting New Churches 139
35 – Mobilizing the Local Church 143
36 – Mobilizing the Local Church: Single Christians 147
37 – Mobilizing the Local Church: Women in God's Service 151
38 – Mobilizing the Local Church: Young Christians 155
39 – Mobilizing the Local Church: Older Christians 159
40 – One Generation Away 163
Epilogue 167
Appendix Articles 171

Preface

I love the local church. It is an important part of God's plan for the spiritual growth and development of His people. He has not left us to serve Him all by ourselves, but has put us into communities of like-minded followers, who seek to honor and praise Him, to reach out to the lost souls in our lives, and to build up (the main Biblical term for this is, to edify) one another.

My goal is for churches to get a copy of this material for each family, and to have the whole church read it together over a 40-day period, and to discuss these ideas together and hopefully, try to change some things in the local church that need to be considered and improved.

I do not travel extensively around the country and certainly not around the world. Still I have been concerned in the last several years, when I have had the opportunity to visit Christians in other places, to see that many congregations are suffering losses of numbers, workers, and morale. Many have resigned themselves to just keeping house for the Lord and not prospering and growing as the Lord intends for His people to do. Saying these things doesn't mean I have been to the congregation where you worship and I am automatically talking about you. There have been many churches that are doing quite well, and from which I have learned some really good things.

Many local churches are struggling mightily. Although nobody in those churches wants this to happen, it is easy for discouragement to set in and for disciples to mentally give up. I want to provide Christians with something to work on, some ideas to incorporate in their collective activities, and some goals to achieve for the glory of God.

I have developed a long list of ideas over the years through the experiences I have had, both good and bad, and I believe will be practical and helpful for others to read about and consider. Everything I write will not work for every individual Christian or for every local church. In certain areas of my work for the Lord, I have had my share of disappointments and failures, as well as some successes. I trust that I have learned from a Biblical perspective, not a worldly one, from both successes and mistakes, and would like to share some of those lessons.

Over the years, I have written a few articles (not many, but some) for gospel magazines published by Christians, which people have responded to in a very positive way. They have written or emailed me to thank me for the things I have written and told me that they hope to utilize some of the ideas in those articles to help strengthen the local church they are a part of. That kind of feedback has always encouraged me greatly. Most of those articles were published in *Biblical Insights*, which is no longer in publication. A few of the articles I will include in this series will be a reprinting of those articles, although I have slightly adapted and expanded some of them; most of the chapters here will be additional thoughts and ideas that I would like to share with others.

I hope you will read these ideas carefully and prayerfully, and I do pray that they will help you and the local church where you are a member. I only want to help.

In Ephesians 4:16, Paul speaks of Christ, "from whom the whole body, joined and knit together by what every joint supplies, according to the effective working by which every part does its share, causes growth of the body for the edifying of itself in love." If each of us, as Jesus followers, will do our part, using our talents and abilities in every circumstance where God gives us opportunities, the local church will grow and prosper.

We often hear prayers that ask the Lord that our work of evangelism will "enlarge the borders of the kingdom," and I hope that we all believe that God can and will answer those prayers. That happens at the local church level, but as each congregation grows and is strengthened, the universal church will grow as well.

It is my desire that these pages will contain helpful information for preachers, shepherds, teachers, and all faithful disciples who wish to serve the Master in an ever greater way.

Obviously, if you want to, you can read through these ideas rather quickly. It shouldn't take that long. But my suggestion is that you read them one per day and then think about them. If you rush through them, they will kind of all run together and not make much impact on your thinking. My idea is for you to read and then meditate on each of the concepts for that day. Then move on to the next principle. Take your time and don't hurry to finish. I think you will find that more meaningful.

Please understand that these thoughts will be my opinion about important Bible subjects. I don't expect anyone to agree with everything I have written. That is fine, and I would be happy to hear from fellow

Christians about these writings, even if you don't agree with what I have suggested. I don't want to get into any ongoing debates with those who might have a different view of these ideas, however. If there is a section with which you disagree, simply skip it and proceed to the next offering.

It should be the desire of every child of God to see the body of Christ grow spiritually and numerically as we faithfully serve Him who loved us and gave His Son to die on the cross for our salvation. May we all seek to love God with all of our heart, soul, mind, and strength and our neighbor as ourselves. If this little book will help us toward that goal, it will have been worth my time to write these ideas.

May God bless each of us as we seek to love, serve, and obey Him. And may we all assemble around His throne some day to praise Him for all eternity.

—Roger Hillis
   rogerhillis1953@gmail.com

Dedication

This book is dedicated to all those godly people who have touched my life with the gospel-preachers, elders, Bible class teachers, my parents, my in-laws, our children and so many other faithful Christians who have helped me to love God and His people.

DAY 1

Time to Rebuild

A general assessment of the current situation among conservative churches of Christ reveals some widespread problems.

- Many churches are shrinking with no plan or prospects to reverse that trend.

- Many Christians are discouraged.

- A lot of churches are growing older and the numbers are smaller and, after a few more funerals, will soon be out of business.

- We face an increasingly secular and immoral society. Moral standards seem to be suffering, even for those who are in the church.

- Young people are leaving the church in large numbers.

- Far too many seem to expect the church to go backward and often look at those churches that are growing with suspicion, as though they must be doing something wrong.

- Many local preachers feel overwhelmed and realize that they just cannot get the job done alone.

Let me state that many churches are doing quite well, and we are grateful to them for their positive example and influence on the rest of us. Keep up the good work.

The churches I have worked with that have grown the most are those that have had the most people in the church working to teach their neighbors. It is just that simple. If it is all left up to the preacher, some growth will occur, but many of those preachers have worked so hard and been appreciated so little at times that many of them are ready to give up if they have not already done so.

An important business principle teaches us that the more contacts we make, the more sales will occur. This same principle applies to gospel work. The Jehovah's Witnesses and Mormons are well aware of this and are willing to endure ridicule and persecution to serve the Lord as they believe they should.

An insurance salesman once approached my father and said, "You don't want to buy any insurance, do you?" If we approach prospects for the gospel with the same attitude, we will end up with the same results. (I understand that we are not "selling" the gospel. This is said to illustrate the Biblical principle of sowing and reaping.)

So what can we do about the situation?

Perhaps the best place to start is by doing what Jesus suggested we do. (That's always a good idea, don't you think?)

"Then He said to His disciples, 'The harvest truly is plentiful, but the laborers are few. Therefore pray the Lord of the harvest to send out laborers into His harvest'" (Matthew 9:37-38).

Is it a regular part of your prayers to God that He would send out more laborers into the harvest? I confess to you that it has not been my consistent practice.

If that's true of you also, why is that? Is it because we don't really care? I don't think that's the case. Is it because we don't believe that the Lord will do what He has promised to do? I don't believe that's it, either. Is it because that kind of prayer would have helped in the first century, but now it won't do much good? We know that is not true as well.

In my case, I fear it is because I have grown weary in well doing (Galatians 6:9). I'm afraid that many of us have lost heart; that much will ever change, no matter what we do. I'm convinced that we don't pray for more laborers because we have believed the lies of Satan that have told us that churches just aren't going to grow much anymore.

We have invited family, friends, or acquaintances to study, and either they haven't been interested or they have not obeyed. So we have concluded, "Nobody is interested in the gospel these days."

We have worked with weak Christians and poured blood, sweat, and tears into their lives only to have them fall away, and we have despaired and said, "What's the use?"

We have tried to encourage other Christians to get to work in personal evangelism or at least set up studies, and when they haven't responded, we have just quit asking.

When we quit trying, the devil wins, and we lose. Is that acceptable?

- Is the gospel still the power of God for salvation or not?

- Is the God of the gospel still in control of the world?

- Are there still souls out there who want to be right with the Lord, but just don't know where to turn?

- Have you prayed for open doors to have more opportunities to preach the truth to lost souls looking for hope?

- Have you prayed for more workers to enter the harvest field, both locally in the church where you worship and worldwide in areas where the gospel still needs to go?

- Do you agree that things could be better? Do you agree that things can get better? Will you agree to do your part to make things better?

Let's begin by praying every day for more workers. If several thousand Christians began to really pray that prayer in faith (James 1:6-8), do you believe the Lord will answer us? I do. Brothers and sisters, it is time to rebuild.

Biblical Insights
September 2010

NOTES

DAY 2

Emphasizing the Basics

Several years ago, a church that had just experienced a division asked me to preach for them. Many members had left, and it was heartbreaking for those who remained. A wise and experienced elder told me, "I've never known a church to grow that didn't emphasize the basics. If a church is struggling, they just need to get back to first principles and preach them like the people have never heard them before." That good advice helped the church to recover and continue to grow.

If Christians do not have a basic understanding of the elementary principles of the gospel, they have no solid foundation on which to build and grow. One of Christ's parables spoke of the need of making certain that we build on the right foundation (see Matthew 7:24-27). That reminds us of the importance of teaching some of the same lessons over and over again.

There are several reasons for this. First, there are always young people growing up who have heard these lessons from the time of their birth. However, at a very young age, most of these studies do not sink in. At some point (and really, only God knows when it will be), a lesson that young people have heard numerous times finally takes hold, and they understand an important truth for the very first time. We should never assume that our young people know and understand Bible subjects just because we know they have heard them before.

Secondly, we can never be sure when a guest will show up and perhaps hear a vital Bible lesson at a crucial time in their life. It may be the first and only time that person will ever have the opportunity to understand an important doctrinal point, one that could make the difference in his eternal destiny. That's also why we should make certain to explain the plan of salvation during a lesson, every time. You just don't know who may be listening carefully and seriously considering obedience. He might have heard many times in the past and done nothing about what he was learning, and still be receptive this time.

Also, we must not assume that our older members (those who have been around a while) can always remember everything they've ever heard. It might have been a long time since they studied a particular subject, or they might be aware of the truth but not know where the verses are that teach that truth. It is always helpful to be reminded of things we know to be true so that our convictions are deep and not easily shaken. These things help to mature and stabilize us spiritually. "...till we all come to the unity of the faith and the knowledge of the Son of God, to a perfect man, to the measure of the stature of the fullness of Christ; that we should no longer be children, tossed to and fro and carried about with every wind of doctrine, by the trickery of men, in the cunning craftiness of deceitful plotting" (Ephesians 4:13-14).

Here is a sample list of the types of sermons that we need to preach at least annually. Of course, we must work hard to present them in a fresh, interesting way, taking a different approach to the same lesson each time.

- Baptism
- Instrumental music
- Distinguishing the covenants
- Bible authority
- Organization of the local church
- Worship of the church
- Work of a local church
- Significance of the Lord's Supper
- Evangelizing the lost
- Strengthening the family
- Silence of the Scriptures
- The power of prayer
- God's grace
- The one, true church
- The cross of Christ

There are probably other topics that should be added to this list. These are merely some of the Bible topics that disciples must be firmly grounded in. "As you have therefore received Christ Jesus the Lord, so walk in Him, rooted and built up in Him and established in the faith, as you have been taught, abounding in it with thanksgiving" (Colossians 2:6-7).

There will be certain subjects that we will never outgrow. We must never be afraid to preach lessons that members have heard many times. When someone has been a Christian for several years, there is almost no way to preach something new to him. As people have said, "If it's new, it isn't true, and if it's true, it isn't new."

Emphasizing the Basics

I'm not suggesting that a preacher should just get one lesson together on baptism and preach it with exactly the same approach to the same people every three months. To stay fresh and vibrant, a preacher needs to restudy, rethink, and restructure his lessons. I have been told that, after he had preached for more than forty years at the Haldeman Avenue church in Louisville, Kentucky, brother M.C. Kurfees was just as fresh in his sermons as when he started. Think about that. To preach for forty years to the same congregation, one would have to continually study and learn new insights from the Bible. If he had four years' worth of sermons and preached them all 10 times, people would have left in large numbers. Instead, the church grew, Christians matured, and the lost were brought to Christ.

No matter how much "strong meat" of the word people can handle, those who are the most mature spiritually will never grow tired of hearing these basic principles of truth, because they know how important they are. They love all truth and do not have to be entertained with "some new thing" all the time.

It might also be helpful for a local church to purchase or write a set of "Bible Basics" material that is taught to all new members. A class like this could be repeated at least one quarter per year (more often if the church is really growing) and use it to help ground new converts in the first principles. Of course, not all sermons should be basic material. Those more mature saints deserve, on some occasions, to hear lessons on some of the more challenging subjects that aren't preached or taught every week. But in a year when most people hear approximately 50-100 sermons, there are plenty of opportunities for both milk and solid food to be taught. "For though by this time you ought to be teachers, you need someone to teach you again the first principles of the oracles of God; and you have come to need milk and not solid food" (Hebrews 5:12).

If people are not growing spiritually, if the church is struggling with carnality and division, if souls are not being saved, look first at the preaching. Maybe we need to just get back to the basics.

Biblical Insights
September 2003

NOTES

DAY 3

A Deliberate Evangelism Strategy

Many churches do not have a deliberate evangelism strategy. Of course, there are notable exceptions. But most churches conduct services, including one or two gospel meetings per year, and hope that members will bring guests (they often do not) or that prospects will happen to show up on their own (this rarely happens either).

Nobody gets too overly concerned that the church isn't growing, but will occasionally change preachers in the hopes that the new man will be just what the church needs to start saving the lost. That is also rare.

Do you know any other area of life where good results just accidentally happen? Where nobody has to plan, organize, and promote, but great things happen anyway?

If you want to raise a nice garden, you have to work at it. You have to prepare the soil, use good seeds, water the growing plants, and pull some weeds along the way. You don't just pick a plot of ground, throw out a bunch of seeds, and then come back in a couple of months ready to eat. It doesn't happen accidentally.

A sports team must practice, exercise, be disciplined, and work on plays together to have a winning season. It doesn't happen accidentally. And the examples could be multiplied.

But sometimes, when it comes to evangelism, we expect results without much effort and without a plan to work. We may occasionally convert someone without a strategy, but we will not experience the kind of growth that we read about in the book of Acts.

One of the jobs of leadership is to give guidance and motivation to those in the group. This is being written primarily for elders, preachers, and men and women of spiritual conviction who have the ability to influence others to do better in the Lord's service. What is your strategy for evangelism? What kind of leadership are you providing in this vital area? What does your example teach?

A deliberate, intentional strategy will include two things: a plan for study and a plan for getting studies.

A plan for study must cover at least three basic truths: a standard for determining what God wants from us, an understanding of sin and how it separates man from God, and the Lord's solution to this sin problem, including our response of obedience. There may be other important lessons that you will want to include or at least study as follow-up material with those who are converted. Still those three principles are the essentials to know before obedience. There are many different study series available that teach these truths, or you can arrange your own. As long as the truth is taught, people will respond. (Not everyone, of course, but many will.)

And we must have a plan for making opportunities to study those principles with the lost. Some have held neighborhood Bible studies in their home and invited everyone who lives close by to attend. It helps if you have established a relationship with your neighbors over time. They are more likely to come to a study if you have been friendly and helpful to them in other ways.

Some have mailed out Bible correspondence courses to everyone living in a certain zip code. A follow-up is required to visit them and set up future opportunities to study with them.

One of the best ways (it is also the most effective, profitable, and inexpensive method) is for members to simply invite their friends, family and acquaintances to study. Many of them will, if we will just ask.

Others have set up booths at county fairs and even the state fair, if you have enough available funds. Give them something to study and something to send back in (like a correspondence course) that will give you their address and phone number to follow up with.

Newspaper articles that teach the truth can often result in Bible studies. Include some material that challenges people's thinking religiously, even to the point of upsetting them because you have touched on some an area especially important to them. They may call you or write you just to defend what they believe. Podcasts can also reach lost souls.

Special services with an important and vital theme, which are widely advertised and announced, can sometimes draw people.

Some disciples have used the website called Meetup.com to set up community Bible studies and Scripture readings in places like restaurants, libraries, and other public facilities. These sessions usually cover a chapter of the Bible per week, or something similar to that. It is a way to introduce interested people to New Testament Christians and the word of God.

Some of these ideas will work better in some areas than in others. In some places, newspaper articles are too expensive; in other areas, they are more affordable. Do something that will be helpful in your particular part of the world.

If you develop a strategy and it doesn't work, try something different. Maybe you will need to keep the parts that work and modify the parts that don't. But do something. Do not quit trying.

What it all boils down to is this: Are we going to be intentional, deliberate, and steadfast in our efforts to teach the lost, or will we be satisfied with doing very little until the church we worship with eventually goes out of business?

Is this our evangelism strategy? "If somebody accidentally wanders into our services, we are ready to teach them." Really? Do you think that is what God meant when He told us to be "steadfast, immovable, always abounding in the work of the Lord?"

Brothers and sisters, think on these things.

Biblical Insights
November 2010

NOTES

DAY 4

Balanced Preaching

"Preach the word! Be ready in season and out of season. Convince, rebuke, exhort, with all longsuffering and teaching. For the time will come when they will not endure sound doctrine, but according to their own desires, because they have itching ears, they will heap up for themselves teachers; and they will turn their ears away from the truth, and be turned aside to fables. But you be watchful in all things, endure afflictions, do the work of an evangelist, fulfill your ministry" (2 Timothy 4:2-5).

Well, that sounds easy enough, doesn't it? Just preach God's word and don't turn aside to other things that would keep you from speaking the truth. Anyone who thinks being a gospel preacher is an easy job has never done it. It is a highly rewarding pursuit, but an extremely challenging one as well.

We are discussing, in this book on *Strengthening the Local Church*, some things that will help Jesus' followers to grow, spiritually in our personal lives and numerically on the congregational level. Sound preaching is vital to both spiritual and numerical growth.

Paul said, "I am not ashamed of the gospel of Christ, for it is the power of God to salvation..." (Romans 1:16). We must learn to preach God's word always, in its purity, without apology and without reservation or compromise.

Luke also records Paul's words for us, in Acts 20:27, in which he reminds the shepherds from Ephesus that he had preached "the whole counsel of God" while in their city. We must preach the Bible in its completeness, both popular and unpopular subjects.

A church will only be as strong, or as weak, as the preaching it receives.

And the pulpit, through the messages that emanate from it, will determine the "tone" or "culture" of the local church. Strong, solid, faithful gospel preaching can raise the commitment level of the entire church, from the weakest disciple to the strongest. It is said that a rising tide raises all ships, and that principle applies spiritually as well as nautically.

Paul told Timothy to convince, rebuke, and exhort with patience and careful instruction. He was not suggesting, as some have said, that our teaching should be two-thirds negative and one-third positive. Paul was reminding his young preaching friend, and it is preserved by inspiration for us today, that there will be a need for both tearing down false ideas and teachings and for building up the truth of God's will among the members of every local church.

Timothy was also encouraged by Paul (1 Timothy 4:16) to watch both his life (how he conducts himself day by day) and his teaching (what he says in the pulpit and the classroom, as well as when he teaches from house to house). Much of the success or weakness of a congregation can be traced directly back to the preaching the church receives.

An evangelist must be friendly and outgoing. That doesn't mean he has to be the life of every party and the chief entertainer of every assembly. It means that guests must feel welcomed when attending our services and be told repeatedly by the members that they are glad the guests came. And while you and I know that the preacher is not more important to God than any other member of the church, those who visit our services will often think otherwise. If he doesn't project warmth and friendliness, many will not feel comfortable returning to hear more. This is just a simple matter of understanding human nature.

Is the preacher evangelistic in his own life? A non-evangelistic preacher is not going to be able to motivate others to really get out there and save the lost if they know he talks about it a lot but does little in this area. (Frankly, is there really even such a thing as a non-evangelistic evangelist? Maybe he should be honest enough to call himself something else if he is not really doing the work of an evangelist.) There must be an emphasis on evangelism that begins in the pulpit, but everyone must see that it reaches beyond those who enter our facilities to include those who have never attended a service or a study. This is one of several areas where the preacher really must practice what he preaches, or no one else will practice it either.

Does the preacher show an interest in young people, older members, and everyone in between? Often, a preacher has a natural tendency to spend more time with those his own age and with whom he shares similar interests. But sometimes this can make others feel unimportant, more like an outsider than a real member of the spiritual family.

There must also be a focus on telling people about Jesus, the Savior of the world. He said of Himself, "And I, if I am lifted up from the earth, will draw all peoples to Myself" (John 12:32). Of course, He was speaking of His crucifixion, but we must lift Him up in our messages and classes as well. Paul said that when he preached in the first-century city of Corinth, "...I determined not to know anything among you except Jesus Christ and Him crucified" (1 Corinthians 2:2). We need to speak constantly of Him. When I began preaching full-time, I decided to deliver a lesson about Christ at least once a month, and often more frequently than that.

Often our preaching is centered around certain truths about the Lord's church, the need for Bible authority, what constitutes Biblical obedience to the Lord (faith, repentance, confession, baptism), how to worship God correctly (especially no instrumental music and being sure to take the Lord's Supper every Sunday), and other similar doctrinal issues. I believe what the Bible says about every one of those matters, and we cannot be faithful to the Lord without a proper understanding and obedience to those important truths. They must be taught regularly.

However, we are not told to simply teach people to accept the truth on an important group of items. We must teach them to love God with all of their heart, soul, mind, and strength and to be converted to Jesus Christ as their Lord and Savior. I believe that a person who is taught to love Christ will also want to know all of the truth that can set them free (John 8:32). But it is also possible to only learn what the Bible says about some key, important issues and not really be in love with Christ.

Gospel preaching must point people to Jesus, who alone can take away their sins and make them right with God (John 14:6). And then, when they become one of His, we can teach them "to observe all things that I have commanded you" (Matthew 28:20).

NOTES

DAY 5

New Convert Follow-Up

Matthew's version of the Great Commission reads like this: "Go therefore and make disciples of all the nations, baptizing them in the name of the Father and of the Son and of the Holy Spirit, teaching them to observe all things that I have commanded you; and lo, I am with you always, even to the end of the age. Amen." (Matthew 28:19-20).

The first part of that assignment (verse 19) pertains to making disciples for Jesus, followers who will commit their lives to Him. This part of the commission is important and is often emphasized that we must convert people to Christ. The second part of the Great Commission (verse 20), however, is just as important, but often is not emphasized as much as the first part. "Teaching them to observe all things that I have commanded you" refers to helping these new Christians to grow spiritually. The term that is often used for this is follow-up.

Many passages deal with this concept of growing stronger in our relationship with Jesus.

"As newborn babes, desire the pure milk of the word, that you may grow thereby" (1 Peter 2:2).

"You therefore, beloved, since you know these things beforehand, beware lest you also fall from your own steadfastness, being led away with the error of the wicked; but grow in the grace and knowledge of our Lord and Savior Jesus Christ. To Him be the glory both now and forever. Amen" (2 Peter 3:17-18).

This growth needs to begin as soon as the new Christian dries off from baptism. And, in the physical realm, who is responsible for the growth of a new baby? Isn't it the ones who brought him into the world? Giving birth is only the beginning of parental responsibility. If a father and mother don't take care of that need, it is looked upon in society as a criminal act of abuse and neglect. But often, in the spiritual realm, we baptize someone into Christ, make sure they have a Bible to read and study, and then move on to the next prospect.

Those of us who help to teach someone the gospel need to stay with them and help them mature in faith after they become disciples of Christ. The Bible uses several words to describe this spiritual growth process: being grounded, rooted, and settled. New Christians are encouraged to develop in the faith and to grow to maturity. The Bible compares this process to that of a new baby growing into adulthood.

Of course, this parallel is not exactly the same, because the new Christians are old enough to have some responsibility for this, as well as those who have taught them. But we must not just assume that they can take care of themselves in every regard now that they have obeyed the gospel. They probably will not realize how important certain things are in helping with their growth.

We have a responsibility to help protect new Christians from those temptations that could lure them away from Christ and back into the world. The parable of the Sower (Luke 8) tells us that some of those who become Jesus' followers will not remain faithful to Him. And Jesus also tells us why they will stumble and fall.

The seed that falls by the wayside (verse 12) will not produce a Christian in the first place because the devil prevents the word of God from even entering their hearts.

The seed that falls on rocky soil produces a new Christian (verse 13), but then they are drawn away by temptations of the world that can include such things as old friends who will try to convince them to quit the Christian life and to continue old bad habits that will not let them go on to spiritual maturity. We need to warn new disciples about these things and provide them with a whole new set of godly friends who can help them overcome the old bad habits (sins) that they used to love.

The seed that falls among thorns (verse 14) represents people who obey the gospel because they want to serve God, but then Satan makes certain that they have problems in their lives, which can cause them to doubt their decision and often, to give up on their newly discovered faith. Verse 14 warns about "the cares of this life." This warning includes things like job or money problems, family concerns, health issues, or any number of other things that may or may not be sinful in and of themselves, but which can distract and discourage new Christians, often causing them to reverse their decision to follow the Lord. (It is no coincidence that the Bible tells us that, immediately after His baptism, Jesus Himself was tempted by the devil; see Matthew 3:13-4:11.)

We must be certain that we warn new Christians of the many ways in which Satan will try to deceive them and convince them to quit serving God. Several things can help stabilize a new convert and assist them in spiritual growth.

Bible studies must continue with this individual. Just because he now knows enough to become a Christian and has done that, this doesn't mean he knows everything he needs to know about serving the Lord. The church can offer regular Bible classes that will enable the Christian to learn more about the Bible, prayer, worship, and other related topics. A course in "Bible Basics" can help the new follower of Christ understand the Bible and how to find answers to the ways Satan will attempt to discourage them from growth and development.

Private Bible studies should continue with the new Christian, and in most cases, it is probably best for the brothers and sisters who taught this one the gospel to stay with the study and help him continue his spiritual journey to heaven. It might be helpful to have others from the local church join some of these follow-up studies so they can become familiar and comfortable in studying with others. Statistics have shown that a new Christian needs at least three members of the church to become friends with, so that they are not tempted to go back to former, worldly friends who might draw them away.

Ask the new Christian to suggest people whom they would like to see become Christians, like family, friends, neighbors, co-workers, fellow students, and others. They will likely want to share their new faith with long-time friends that we would not have a chance to know otherwise. They may set up more Bible studies with non-Christians that will result in even more conversions.

Invite new Christians into your home for a meal and, perhaps, a short Bible study. Get to know them and let them get to know you as well. The first-century Christians spent a lot of time together outside of their assemblies (Acts 2:44-46; Acts 4:32), and this helped the new disciples to be close to one another.

NOTES

DAY 6

Expecting the Preacher to Do Everything

Years ago, many Christians were opposed to a church hiring a full-time preacher. Their concern (in many cases) was not that the practice was unbiblical, but simply that it might be unwise. They were afraid that, if the church had a full-time, paid minister, too many Christians would just stop doing much of anything and expect the paid preacher to do it all.

Some referred to this as the "paid pastor" system or the "one man pastor" system. This full-time, paid position was especially a concern for churches that did not have elders.

We have all heard the description of many churches that says, the preacher does the work of the elders, the elders do the work of deacons and the deacons and other members do little or nothing. Have you ever known of congregations that could be described in that way?

There will always be people who expect others to do their work for them. That is true in the workplace, often in the home, and in almost every circumstance in life. It can also be true of a local church.

Many jobs often fall to the preacher.

- Visit all the members in the hospital or who are sick at home
- Teach all of the adult Bible classes
- Take people to the doctor
- Run someone to the grocery store
- Be the social director who plans all the get-togethers
- Organize the teaching program
- Order all of the class material
- Recruit all the children's teachers
- Mediate family disputes
- Change the church sign
- Pacify the critics
- Teach all of the prospects
- Encourage the weak
- Shoulder the blame if the church isn't growing
- Send gospel meeting announcements to area churches

- Mow the lawn
- Clean the building
- Write the bulletin articles – type, print, fold, etc.
- Be responsible for the newspaper or other advertising
- Follow up with all the guests

I am not suggesting that it is wrong for the preacher to do anything on this list, but I am saying that it is wrong for a church to expect the preacher to do everything on the list while others do nothing. And if he does some of these things, the congregation should understand that he does most of them because he is a Christian and not because it is part of his work as the preacher or because he doesn't have anything else to do.

People have often said, "That's what we pay him for." And some of the things on this list should rightly be considered to be the work of an evangelist. But the idea that many have expressed that it must be nice to have a job where you only work two days a week, Sunday and Wednesday, displays little real understanding of the Bible description of a preacher's work. Most preachers I know do not do too little work, but many of them are expected to do too much.

This may explain why there are preachers who burn out trying to do too much and quit preaching. Have you ever known a gospel preacher who quit preaching full-time? Have you wondered why?

A preacher needs some time to recharge and refresh himself personally and spiritually. He needs adequate time off for personal or family vacation time and for additional learning opportunities, such as attending lectureships or a special series of Bible studies at another congregation.

Does the preacher ever get to sit in a Bible class and learn from others? Do other men of the church take a turn filling the pulpit every once in a while so he can listen to the gospel rather than always being the one to deliver it?

There are times when serving God full-time can be overwhelming and make a person feel like they are doing it alone. Elijah felt that way (1 Kings 19), and although God reminded him that he was not the only faithful servant in Israel, He gave Elijah forty days off to go into the wilderness and refresh himself for the days ahead (verse 8).

Expecting the Preacher to Do Everything

A friend of mine commented recently in a Bible class that her father, who is an elder in the Lord's church, has often said that a preacher gets too much credit when things go well and too much blame when things go wrong.

The Bible teaches that every member of the body of Christ is important and has a vital function to perform in the work of a local church (see 1 Corinthians 12:12-31 and Ephesians 4:11-16). The truth is that many Christians expect the preacher to do far more than God expects of him and, as a result, those Christians often do far less than the Lord expects them to do.

A church where everyone else sits back and does little or nothing and expects the preacher to do all of the work (because that's what we pay him to do) is going to fail. We are a team, working together to serve God, to defeat the devil, and to win souls for the Lord.

The apostle Paul wrote, in Philippians 1:27, "Only let your conduct be worthy of the gospel of Christ, so that whether I come and see you or am absent, I may hear of your affairs, that you stand fast in one spirit, with one mind striving together for the faith of the gospel." The phrase translated as "striving together" is an athletic term that speaks of brothers and sisters in the Lord working as a team to accomplish the work that He has given all of us to do—together.

The song says, "There is much to do; there's work on every hand." Let's all put our hands to the plow (as Jesus describes in Luke 9:62) and do the work God has assigned all of His children to do. The church will grow, souls will be saved, God will be glorified, and the preacher can be happy and fulfilled as he devotes his life to "the work of the Lord" (1 Corinthians 15:58).

NOTES

DAY 7

Developing A Quality Teaching Program

It is fair to assume that most people who attend Bible classes and worship services on a regular basis do so because of their desire to know the Bible better and, therefore, to learn how to obey God and serve Him. Even for guests who may not realize how important the Bible is, we need to be teaching them the word of God.

All Christians need to grow spiritually, and young people need to learn God's word; both of those things happen the same way, through Bible study, in our private lives and corporately, in the teaching program at the church. (Much learning should also take place at the home and family level, and both private and public Bible study can work together in that way.)

"Therefore, laying aside all malice, all deceit, hypocrisy, envy, and all evil speaking, as newborn babes, desire the pure milk of the word, that you may grow thereby" (1 Peter 2:1-2).

"But also for this very reason, giving all diligence, add to your faith virtue, to virtue knowledge, to knowledge self-control, to self-control perseverance, to perseverance godliness, to godliness brotherly kindness, and to brotherly kindness love. For if these things are yours and abound, you will be neither barren nor unfruitful in the knowledge of our Lord Jesus Christ" (2 Peter 1:5-8).

"You therefore, beloved, since you know this beforehand, beware lest you also fall from your own steadfastness, being led away with the error of the wicked; but grow in the grace and knowledge of our Lord and Savior Jesus Christ. To Him be the glory both now and forever. Amen" (2 Peter 3:17-18).

"And the things that you have heard from me among many witnesses, commit these to faithful men who will be able to teach others also" (2 Timothy 2:2).

"But you must continue in the things which you have learned and been assured of, knowing from whom you have learned them, and that from childhood you have known the Holy Scriptures, which are able to make you wise for salvation through faith which is in Christ Jesus. All Scripture is given by inspiration of God, and is profitable for doctrine, for reproof, for correction, for instruction in righteousness, that the man of God may be complete, thoroughly equipped for every good work" (2 Timothy 3:14-17).

Many Christians have been in the church for a long time, some for almost their entire lives, and still have not studied certain parts of the Bible (especially in the Old Testament) in an organized Bible class with a qualified teacher. This lack of study should be a matter of concern for those who lead local churches, whether they are elders or those who have to lead in the absence of elders.

You have to be able to help new Christians and teach them to grow and develop spiritually in their knowledge of the Bible and in their relationship with God. It is helpful to have a plan for how you are going to accomplish that important work (the Bible calls it edification).

Every local church needs an organized teaching program that is planned out and is not random or accidental. It should also be flexible enough to change to meet specific needs that will arise both for young people and in the lives of those of us who are older.

We need to teach the whole church what is said in the whole Bible and then take that same message to a lost and dying world. We can make a difference in people's lives and in their eternity. Every Bible class has the potential to take someone who is headed for hell and point them toward heaven. We need to teach others to love Jesus the way we love Him, with all of our heart, soul, mind, and strength.

There are several organized programs that Christians have developed over the years, and many churches rely heavily on these curricula to spiritually educate their members. Other churches have developed their own schedules, and some are hybrids of available commercial material combined with content written by local members.

There are difficulties with a schedule of this type. Singings, weather emergencies, special meetings, etc., sometimes cause classes to be missed. The teacher must be able to catch up by covering the material in fewer weeks. Workbooks and other printed literature are not all equal in quality. Some are excellent and some are not. Some of the literature may be out of print at various times. But, even with the problems, a planned curriculum is much more effective than a haphazard method of study or no method at all. The advantages far outweigh the disadvantages.

Suggestions to consider

- If it is possible, teachers should be alternated regularly. If enough teachers are available, those who teach in one year's classes should be allowed to rest the next year. Of course, smaller churches have fewer teachers to work with, and some may have to teach on a regular basis until the church grows and new teachers are added to the number.

- When using a workbook or class outline, consider these thoughts:

- Every part of the lesson does not have to be read word for word, every question does not have to be answered, and even every scripture does not have to be read in class. A good teacher will use the text, questions, and scriptures that will be the most helpful to the class.

- Never forget that you are studying the Bible, not the workbook. The workbook is only an aid to Bible study.

Goals of the Curriculum

Here are some ideas about the goals that we should want to reach in developing a structured, quality teaching program in the local church.

1. To help people grow to be more like Jesus Christ (1 Peter 2:21)

2. To teach the entire word of God (Acts 20:27)

3. To instill a sense of "doing" (James 1:22)

4. To develop positive attitudes about the word of God and how it applies to everyday life (Philippians 4:8)

5. To develop each person's individual faith and conviction (Romans 10:17) and love for God and Christ

You can reword these principles or come up with your own goals, but the idea is to teach people to love and obey God and His word. Let me know if I can help in some way.

NOTES

DAY 8

How Do You Invite?

The Lord Jesus Christ offered this invitation. "Come to Me, all you who labor and are heavy laden, and I will give you rest. Take My yoke upon you and learn from Me, for I am gentle and lowly in heart, and you will find rest for your souls. For My yoke is easy and My burden is light" (Matthew 11:28-30). He simply invited people to "come."

When two disciples began to follow Christ, they asked Him where He was staying. His answer was uncomplicated: "Come and see" (John 1:38-39). He invited them to "come."

When Philip heard the Lord and went to tell Nathanael that he had found the Messiah, Nathanael asked, "Can anything good come out of Nazareth?" And Philip said to him, "Come and see" (John 1:46). Philip asked Nathanael to "come."

The Samaritan woman became convinced through her personal discussion of spiritual matters with Jesus that He was truly the Messiah. She went back to her friends and acquaintances and told them, "Come, see a Man who told me all things that I ever did. Could this be the Christ?" (John 4:29). She just invited those closest to her to "come."

The New Testament ends with a similar offer. "And the Spirit and the bride say, 'Come!' And let him who hears say, 'Come!' And let him who thirsts come. And whoever desires, let him take the water of life freely" (Revelation 22:17).

All too often, we want to take what is very simple and make it much more complex. We read books like "How to Win Friends and Influence People." We study the latest sales techniques to figure out more clever ways to package the gospel. We bring in the latest "Personal Evangelism" specialist in the brotherhood for a weekend gospel meeting. And, all of that is fine. There can be some value to those approaches.

But the bottom line is really that we just have to invite them. We have to learn how to overcome our reservations and fears and just open our mouths around our friends, neighbors, co-workers, family members, fellow students, and ask them to "come." This is one of those areas of life where, when all is said and done, too often much more is said than done.

The most successful efforts we will make along these lines are with those we know well. "Cold call" selling is not very productive in the business world, although this does work occasionally. Knocking on doors in a given neighborhood may produce a few meager results (hence, the unflagging zeal of our Mormon and Jehovah's Witness friends). But, by far, the people we know and have already developed a relationship with are going to be our best "prospects" for reaching with the gospel.

But, at some point, we just have to swallow hard and say to them, "Come and see."

There are some practical suggestions we can make to help you develop this courage.

- Be yourself. Don't try to come up with some fancy, slick-sounding sales presentation. A simple, "I'd love to have you come to our services this Sunday," is really all you need. When you are friends with someone, it will be harder for them to turn you down than to throw away a flyer from the church that they get in the mail.

- Use special services, like gospel meetings or Vacation Bible School, to invite. Let them know the theme of the week or the specific topic on particular nights. Tell them, "We are going to have a sermon this Tuesday evening that I think will help you as a parent to train your children in the right way. I know I need that, and I'd like for you to hear it also."

- If they don't come to that service, follow up by handing them a CD of the sermon and say, "I know you couldn't make it the other night, so I made you a copy of the lesson. Give it a listen and let me know what you think." And then, be sure to follow up on that. Let them know regularly when a class or sermon would be useful for them. Don't be pushy, but do be persistent.

- Mention the church's website or Face Book page and point out some of the things on it that might help them spiritually.

- Be excited about the local church where you are a member. Mention exciting things that happen from time to time. If you can show them the difference that being a member of Christ's church has made in your life, maybe they will realize that there is something good for them there also.

We need to just focus on those we know and love. They will appreciate our sincerity; they have seen our lives up close for years, and they will not think we are inviting them out of some impure motive.

Three words might be all it takes to set someone on a path that will lead them to heaven. Three words can change an eternal destiny. Three words can save more souls than we can ever imagine. "Come and see."

Biblical Insights
January 2009

NOTES

DAY 9

Effective Gospel Meetings

For those who have grown up around churches of Christ, the term, gospel meeting, will be a familiar one. However, for those who grew up with a denominational background or no religious history at all, this term will not have much meaning.

In the past, churches would have a series of gospel messages in consecutive evening (and/or morning) meetings. So, the phrase "gospel meeting" refers to an effort to preach the gospel to both the church and any unbelievers that Christians could convince to attend. Some denominations (and perhaps some faithful churches as well) used the term, revival, to describe such meetings, as the hope was to renew and encourage a new sense of spiritual commitment to God.

Years ago, many churches did not have a full-time paid preacher who spoke almost every Sunday. A lot of churches (but not all) in the southern and central Illinois area where I grew up would only have "preaching services" one or maybe two Sundays per month. On other Sundays, the church would meet for Bible study and then have a short worship service that would include the Lord's Supper, a short talk by one of the men, and then everyone would go home until next week.

But once a year, the church would have a gospel meeting. It would often be held in the Summer months because many of the members were farmers and they were busy planting in the Spring and harvesting in the Fall. Winter always threatened bad weather, so the Summer months were usually the best time to have such an effort. In the early and middle parts of the twentieth century, such meetings would be two to three weeks or even a month or more long, if the interest remained high. People didn't have as many distractions as we seem to have now. It was not uncommon for these long meetings to include many sincere people who would visit from their denominational churches. When they heard the truth, many of those who were genuinely seeking the truth would respond in obedience. If you invited family, friends, and neighbors, many of them would attend. Even among the local families in the church, some people would wait until the gospel meeting to be baptized, and so it was not uncommon to hear of gospel meetings that would last a month and scores of people would be baptized into Christ.

When I was just getting started trying to preach, I preached for a while at a small church in central Illinois one Sunday per month. Different members would tell me on Sunday afternoon when it was their turn to feed the preacher about the gospel meeting in the 1970's when 13 young people were baptized on the same night. Although they didn't have 13 young people attending any more when I was preaching there, their dream was always to repeat the success of that one meeting.

As people's schedules got fuller and busier, churches began to shorten the length of gospel meetings, but perhaps have two per year, one in the Spring and another in the Fall. Most meetings started on Monday night and went through the following Sunday. Then they switched from Sunday to Friday, and now, many meetings run from Sunday to Wednesday (or maybe Tuesday). And of course, we now try to encourage people not to wait for anything once they are convinced they need to be baptized. So most people aren't even baptized during a regular service time, but many are immersed during the week as soon as they know they shouldn't put it off.

We have very few baptisms these days in gospel meetings (although every one that we do have is important and precious in the sight of God). I do not have any scientific research to back up this statement, but I have noted, in the places I have worshiped, that more meetings have no baptisms than those that may have one or two. I am not writing this to convince us to quit having meetings, but there are a few things we can do to make them more effective.

First, although some preachers will think I am speaking blasphemy, perhaps in some cases, we should not call them gospel meetings. I say that only because most of our unsaved friends won't know what we mean if we invite them to a gospel meeting. Of course, we can explain it to them, and if they come, that is great. However, it is just as appropriate to call them a teaching seminar, a Bible lectureship, or, as a friend of mine likes to call them, a guest speaker series. We only refer to them as gospel meetings by tradition (the phrase 'gospel meeting' is not found in the Bible), and perhaps a different designation might spark more interest and attract more sincere people seeking the truth. This is just something we might consider.

Secondly, we should ask ourselves what we want to accomplish with this series of Bible lessons. Because our members' schedules (and those of our lost friends) are so busy, we need to be wise about the time it takes to attend a week-long series (or even one night for some people). Let's use the time wisely. Isn't that what Ephesians 5:16 and Colossians 4:5 teach us? Make it really worth their while to attend by having a theme or series of lessons that speak directly to their everyday lives, and then show them how that applies to their eternity as well.

Maybe we can use the time as a focused, intensive study time on a particular subject or a book or series of books from the Bible. Perhaps we should have fewer meetings but make them more targeted times of Bible instruction.

Several years ago, I was away at a gospel meeting, and my wife received a phone call from the preacher at another church, where I was scheduled to speak in about a month. He told her they didn't really have a theme in mind, but they wanted me to preach lessons that would appeal to non-Christians. That's a great idea, of course, one I highly recommend, and so she asked him if they typically had a lot of non-Christians attend their meetings. He admitted they almost never had anyone to visit their meetings, and so she asked him if they were doing something different this time that might attract non-believers to this meeting. Again, he said no, so she kindly and politely asked him why they wanted me to preach sermons for non-Christians if they weren't going to be there? He told her that they just hoped that maybe this time, some might come. (That was in 1986; we had about 250 souls there on Sunday morning, and now, many years later, that church has about twenty in attendance on a good Sunday morning.)

Wouldn't it make more sense to preach to the people who typically come to such services or to have a theme or study that might appeal to those who didn't normally attend? However, to just randomly preach lessons that would help unbelievers if they were there, in the empty hope that they might accidentally show up, is not wise.

We cannot afford to waste the Lord's money and the efforts, energy, time, and goodwill of the members, just because fifty years ago, we had a gospel meeting and a dozen people were baptized. Times have changed, haven't they? Without changing the message, we need to change the methods we are using to spread the best news in the universe to those who desperately need it.

NOTES

DAY 10

Using Social Media for the Church

The influence of social media has become a reality that churches cannot afford to ignore.

It is true that there are many people in the world who are using social media for ungodly purposes, but that does not mean we should neglect to realize the potential for good that social media holds. It is more than just vapid pictures of vain people who are trying to show off and show out. The entire internet has great potential to help us reach lost souls with the gospel of Christ. Perhaps some will even hear, learn, and obey the truth because of the social media teaching that we can do. If we use it carefully and properly, the internet can be a wonderful tool for a local church to spread the good news of salvation. But we must use it in a godly and appropriate way.

Many of us have gone to restaurants and noticed a table with 4-6 people sitting around it, each of them using their mobile phone to ignore the other people at the table. Electronic devices have taken over our culture, and we should figure out ways we can capitalize on opportunities to use these platforms for the spreading of the kingdom of God.

There are various forms of social media, and many of them can be utilized to teach the truth. Some of them are free and will cost the church little or no money if there is someone in the church who can access these forums. If the church has someone with at least minimal computer experience, perhaps someone from a neighboring congregation can help to set up and show how to operate some of the available avenues.

The difficulty of listing specific social media platforms is that things change so quickly in this realm. In the music industry, things began with vinyl records, then eight-track tapes, then cassettes, and finally compact discs (CDs). The most recent (as of November 2025) are streaming services where you do not physically own a copy of a song, album, or movie. Still, you have to pay individually or as part of a subscription to download or listen to a song or watch a movie. The world is changing quite rapidly, and it is not within my abilities to foresee where things might be going in the future. I hope, as we talk about the use of social media, that you will realize that, although the specific platforms may (and most likely will) change, we can learn principles about how to spread the gospel, using whatever technology clever humans might come up with, sometimes sooner rather than later.

Magazines that teach gospel lessons were, at one time, a primary source of spreading the word of God to others. Historians talk about how influential these magazines were. Most families of Christians would subscribe to at least one magazine, often several, and would benefit greatly from them. Many of them began as weekly publications, then monthly, and some quarterly. While a few are still available in print, most of the ones that still exist are online. Many of the old-time favorites have completely stopped publishing, while others are still trying to make good teaching available for those who are interested.

Let's talk about a few of the currently available methods for teaching that we might consider using for the work of the local church. I am not an expert on any of these formats, but I have learned just a little about some of them.

Websites
This is a huge step forward in making the church's existence known to the digital world. I would guess that more churches have websites than those that don't, but that doesn't mean they are all of equal quality or effectiveness. The information on a church website needs to be biblical, relevant, up to date, and helpful to those who are searching for truth. There is usually a charge for having a website online, and someone in the church needs to be tech-savvy enough to do the behind-the-scenes work of posting, editing, and answering questions that might come from visitors to the website.

Facebook
This platform can be helpful in spreading the gospel. Some churches have used Facebook Live to broadcast services for those unable to attend in person, then posted the lessons for others to watch later. Facebook is also a helpful format in which to announce events, like Vacation Bible School, gospel meetings, lectureships, singings, etc. Many churches also announce Bible class information and weekly sermon titles in an attempt to create interest in those who might attend.

YouTube
Many churches are now recording their sermons and classes and posting them online for others to watch and learn. Again, the church needs

at least one member who has the knowledge of (or the willingness to learn) how to do this. Podcasts can also be used to teach Bible lessons.

Email lists
Many churches use email to communicate with their members and sometimes, with others as well. Some send out articles, information updates, and other learning opportunities. Some churches that formerly mailed out their teaching bulletin are now sending it out electronically. It would be helpful to have a separate list for members and one for others.

There are other platforms, including TikTok, Instagram, Twitter (now called X), Pinterest, and Snapchat. Some of these may well go out of business, change their names, or be replaced by the latest trends or fads, but many of them are similar, and there will be both good and bad characters who will take advantage of these opportunities to spread a message. Our message on any or all of these programs should contain the potential to change someone's eternal destiny. God works through our efforts.

Here are some suggestions about social media. These principles generally apply to any platform that you might choose.

Don't be afraid to quote the Bible. Some will not accept the Bible as inspired by God, but we believe it is and that the gospel is the power of God for the salvation of souls (Romans 1:16). So we must not be ashamed to show people that we believe in and trust the Bible. Specific teaching articles that point people to Jesus as the Savior are helpful in this context.

Use images and pictures in addition to words. Pictures of people in Bible class or the congregation standing for a song, heads bowed in prayer, and a preacher reading from the word of God can reinforce our claim to be people of the book.

The internet is not going away. It will continue to be an influence in our lives, for good or for ill. We have been presented with the possibility to use it in a good way.

NOTES

DAY 11

What if the Church Isn't Growing?

There may be any number of reasons why churches in some areas of this country and around the world are not growing.

I do not want in any way to imply that, if a local church isn't growing, then the group is not pleasing to God. They may be doing something wrong that displeases God, but numerical growth, or lack of it, is not a singular indicator either way. It is not my purpose in this series to imply that all a church has to do to grow spiritually and numerically is to follow my advice. This is not intended to be a fool-proof, works every time, money-back-guaranteed program.

These chapters are simply things I have observed over the years that have helped some churches to grow. It is my desire that these articles encourage some Christians who have grown despondent and believe that nothing can be done to help struggling churches to develop hope for the future. The last thing I want to do is to discourage the downhearted further.

Sometimes things just don't work out the way we had hoped they would.

- Noah preached (2 Peter 2:5) for 100 years and didn't save anyone outside of his family. He had to have been discouraged at times. But he did save his own family. And that is awesome.

- In Acts, Paul did not have equally glowing success in every place where he went to plant a new church. In some places, he was ignored; in some, he was thrown into prison; in some, he was stoned or otherwise persecuted. (Read 2 Corinthians 11:22-30).

- And, lest we forget, even the Savior Himself did not convince everyone He taught to become His followers. As a matter of fact, He was killed by some of the very people He tried to teach.

- And sometimes, despite of our best efforts, we work very hard with little visible results.

Strengthening the Local Church

Many factors can lead to a church that is shrinking in size, rather than growing. Churches age (because all of us as people do also), sickness and death occur, people move away from a community, and the culture of an entire city or town can be affected by outside influences. All of these things can have a shrinking effect on the Lord's people. Some places are just harder fields to work in than others are.

Churches go through cycles, sometimes up and sometimes down, and it can be difficult to know if a downturn in attendance is part of a cycle that is beyond anyone's control or whether it is evidence of a decline that will ultimately lead to the death of that church.

One of the easiest things churches often do is blame the preacher if things start to go badly. It may be that he is the problem, and I am convinced that most churches need to do a better and more thorough job of choosing a preacher. More time should be spent finding out if the churches where he has worked before have grown spiritually and numerically, or if they have declined in number. Sometimes they decline, and it isn't his fault, but some preachers systematically destroy every church they work with. They don't mean to, but they don't have a very realistic view of themselves that will allow them to admit that they hurt the church more than they help it. Not everyone who preaches should be preaching, but it is hard for most men to admit that they are the problem, and the churches that have been in decline would have grown if someone else had been preaching there.

My family attended a church once while we were on vacation, and the preacher told me that they were getting ready to move to a newer and smaller building. He said, "We've grown so small here that we don't need this much space." We've grown so small? That is an interesting way to describe a church that is dying. I am afraid even to try to find out if that church is meeting at all now, about twenty five years later.

Before I give a few suggestions about what to do in this type of situation, please allow me to give a word of warning about what not to do.

Do not turn to gimmicks, games, entertainment, and other unbiblical "methods" to draw a crowd. It can be tempting to try something that the big denominational group down the road is doing that has resulted in huge crowds attending there now. Never forget that the gospel is God's power to save (Romans 1:16), and while "food, fun, and fellowship" may well attract bigger numbers, they will not save souls.

But what we can do sometimes is to try to find different ways to reach the lost with the gospel than we have used in the past, without changing the message. We can look for better, Biblically authorized ways to do what God wants us to do.

I have previously suggested going back to the basics of the gospel to try to ground the members you already have and encourage them to share the truth with their lost friends and neighbors.

A suggestion I have made to churches that are disheartened (to help them not give up) is for every Christian to take an entire year and focus on one lost person. Then pray for that person, spend social time getting to know him better, and when the opportunity arises, invite him to attend a service or to have a Bible study at his convenience, wherever he would be willing. Just concentrate on one person for a whole year. If a church of twenty people were to do that and not drop the ball, but stay on task, in one year the church would be forty people. And then, if everyone chose one person for the next year and stay with him, the second year, there would be eighty people. And, if they all did it again for another year, after only three years, those original twenty members would number 160 members. After four years, you would have 320 members and after five years, 640. Now, of course, some would move away, some would pass away, some would fall away, but is it that difficult to think about spending a whole year working on one lost soul, to bring him or her to the Lord?

Acts 14:21 says, "And when they had preached the gospel to that city and made many disciples, they returned to...(other cities)." That's how it works, friends. We preach the gospel to people, and it results in new disciples. If your garden isn't producing as many fresh tomatoes as you want, you plant more tomato seeds. If the church isn't producing new Christians, it must plant more gospel seeds.

How long has it been since you personally met and taught someone who became a Christian? Ten years? Five years? One year? Twenty five years? Have you ever done that? It isn't that hard; we just have to stay with it. So whatever else you do, don't quit trying. Don't give up. Lost souls, who need the Lord, are out there, everywhere. They need you to keep trying to reach them. Their eternal destiny is on the line here.

"And let us not grow weary while doing good, for in due season we shall reap if we do not lose heart" (Galatians 6:9). Don't grow weary and do nothing. Never give up.

NOTES

DAY 12

Helping Young Men to be Spiritual Leaders

How many times have you heard that young people are the church of the future? This statement is true, but this will be effective only if we are already using them and developing them into leaders now. "The father of the righteous will greatly rejoice, he who fathers a wise son will be glad in him" (Proverbs 23:24, ESV).

Starting Early

Basically, leadership is simply influence over others. Early on, we need to help our young people develop the strength of character to be "influence leaders" among their peers, leaders rather than simply followers. Sermons and Bible classes need to emphasize God's truth on subjects concerning moral issues, character qualities, and having the right kind of attitudes. "Train up a child in the way he should go, and when he is old he will not depart from it" (Proverbs 22:6).

The single most important thing to teach our young people is the proper respect they should have for authority. Initially, they learn this respect at home in their relationship with their parents. Later, it is reflected among other adults, including family friends, Bible class teachers, neighbors, school teachers, and others at school. They need to be taught to behave politely and to answer properly. "Yes or no, sir or ma'am" should be the standard response, not "yeah" or "nope." They should be taught to respect property and to act on the first statement, not after several empty threats. Children will be children, of course, but they need to learn early in life to be obedient children. Respect for others in authority makes it easier for a person to develop respect for God and His authority.

As children grow into adolescence, their knowledge of the Bible should grow as well. Hopefully, the congregation will have an active and comprehensive Bible class program that will fill them with both a complete knowledge of God's word and a heart of love for the Lord that will serve them well throughout life. However, the primary responsibility for the spiritual development and nurturing of children was not given to the church, but to the parents, especially the father (Ephesians 6:4). Bible classes conducted by the church should only supplement the teaching they get at home, not replace it. Unfortunately, we all know of situations where all the Bible children learn is what they get "at church." That emphasizes the importance of a well-organized teaching program in each congregation.

We also cannot overstate the importance of adults providing the best possible example for young people. It does little good for the Sunday morning teacher to tell our children the need to put God first in all things if that teacher doesn't even attend mid-week services. Most important in this area is the example that young people learn at home. The good teaching and preaching that many young people receive is often undone in the car on the way home. Very few of these young people will grow up to be strong leaders in the church.

When young men obey the gospel, they need to be worked into the public services of the church at a rate with which they can be comfortable. They should not be pushed, but often do need to be encouraged to use and develop their talents. I would never have agreed to lead singing if one elder had not stayed with me and helped me to see that this was something I could do if I only would.

Young men's training classes can be very helpful in this area. When conducted properly, with a positive tone and encouraging suggestions, young men (and maybe some older ones also) can be helped to understand the extent of what they can do for the Lord. And beyond the typical classes on song leading, Bible reading, praying publicly, and waiting on the Lord's table, classes need to be held on leadership, what makes a leader, what a leader does, problems a leader faces, qualifications of elders, etc.

At a congregation where I formerly preached, I used to make a Wednesday night talk once a year on the subject of Preparing Young Men for the Eldership. Here are the points I discussed in that short lesson.

Some Practical Steps

Do not wait until you are forty or fifty years old and then decide that you might like to serve as an elder. Start now to think about it and work toward this commendable goal for the rest of your life.

1. Learn the Word.
   Titus 1:9 speaks of the importance of being able to convict those who oppose truth. The only way to do that is to know the truth yourself.

Be serious in your Bible classes. Have fun, but don't forget why you are there. The purpose of Bible classes is to transform your life for eternity. An elder must be "able to teach." You can't teach what you don't know.

2. Maintain a Life of Purity.
Shepherds are to be held in high esteem by others both inside and outside the church. Don't do foolish things that people will remember and that can haunt you for the rest of your life. 1 Timothy 4:12 reminds young people to set a good example for other believers. Use your talents now; do not wait until you get older to start serving.

3. Marry a Godly Woman (1 Timothy 3:11).
Your mate can help you to qualify as an elder, or could be a permanent disqualification. Choose wisely. Young ladies should try to qualify themselves to be elder's or preacher's wives, to be the kind of person a leader can rely on as a helper.

4. Read the Elders' Qualifications Often and Grow in Needed Areas.
You will not develop these leadership qualities accidentally or overnight. They are found in 1 Timothy 3:1-7; Titus 1:6-9; and 1 Peter 5:1-4.

Parents need to encourage their sons to work toward being elders (or gospel preachers). Others can be a great encouragement to young people, also. There is no greater service we can do for the Lord than to help young people grow and develop into spiritual leaders of the church of the future.

Biblical Insights
April 2004

NOTES

DAY 13

A New Evangelistic Idea

All right, it's not totally new (Ecclesiastes 1:9). However, I don't hear many people discussing it these days. Everyone always seems to be looking for the latest gimmick or scheme for church growth. We have filmstrips, videos, lesson plans, and suggestions galore. And, as long as they teach the truth, it really doesn't matter which one you might be the most comfortable using.

But, may I suggest going back to a really old idea? Maybe it's time to resurrect something that has worked for us in the past.

Why don't we try to bring our lost friends and neighbors to our services so they can hear the gospel, be convicted by it, and obey God's plan for the salvation of their souls?

Now, be honest. How long has it been since you personally brought a friend or neighbor with you to the regular worship services of the local church you are a part of? I don't mean a Christian visiting from out of town, but a real-life, bona fide sinner who needs to hear the gospel?

Some churches have had a "bring your neighbor" day with a special emphasis on doing just that. You may not be totally comfortable with that idea, and yet, it does provide a format for those who are shy to invite their friends. That's really the same principle as a gospel meeting. It is designed to be a "bring your neighbor" week; we just don't call it that.

However, it seems to me that we have all but quit trying to bring lost people to gospel meetings. We want them to come. But, they usually don't. We expend lots of time, effort, and money on a meeting. And we are satisfied if one or two guests show up all week long. In the last gospel meeting where you attend, how many non-Christians did you personally invite? We often expect someone else to bring the guests. We are really disappointed if no one comes. But how much did we do toward getting non-Christians there? We either need to work at having a successful meeting or stop wasting everybody's time, money, and energy.

The principle of sowing and reaping (Galatians 6:7) teaches us that the results are proportionate to our efforts. In other words, if we continue to do the same things in the same way we have always done them, we will continue to get the same results. No one will come. If you think that's acceptable, that's between you and the Lord. But if you don't think it's enough, then we need to come up with a plan to do better.

Here's a suggestion.

Plan your regular services in advance. Choose important sermons and coordinate the songs to go along with the lesson. Announce the sermon title at least a week in advance.

This will give everyone an opportunity to say to their friends, "Say, the lesson this week at services is going to be something I think you will really enjoy. We'd love to have you come." Is that so hard? Can't everyone do this?

This has the additional advantage of giving our guests the chance to hear the regular preacher, the one they will hear each week if they become a member. Often, they get excited about a gospel meeting preacher, and then he goes back home, and the person they hear at their next visit is someone very different. That doesn't hurt anything, I guess, but it can set up false expectations and some degree of disappointment on their part.

I recognize that announcing sermons a week or a month ahead will require more organization on the part of the local preacher. And there will be times when the needs of the moment may require choosing a different sermon than the one previously announced. But the extra effort will be well rewarded.

There are helpful ways that this idea can be organized.

It might be (and this is a fairly popular plan) that the preacher decides to preach a series of lessons that are all connected by a common theme. It might be a series of lessons on Bible Basics. Here, the preacher would preach several sermons in a row on the primary aspects of important scriptural subjects that he believes everyone ought to know and understand. It would be helpful, when finishing one lesson, to announce to everybody what the next step or study in this series will be.

A New Evangelistic Idea

Maybe the speaker will decide to preach a series of lessons on the life of Christ. Not a detailed study of every verse in Matthew, Mark, Luke, and John, but 8 or 10 or 12 (or 4) studies about highlights of Jesus and His life. Again, after one study, announce what will be talked about next week.

Or maybe the preacher likes to emphasize textual studies over topical lessons. So maybe he will want to preach a lesson on each chapter from the book of Acts, for example. For 28 weeks, everyone can know that, whichever chapter he preaches about today, Lord willing, the sermon for next week will cover the next chapter, until all of them have been studied together. If a preacher works long enough with one church, he might eventually preach his way through the entire Bible, or at least through the New Testament.

My point is that, if this is done in an organized way, the whole church can realize not only that they are going to study their way through the Bible, but also that they can use this knowledge to invite others who are not Christians to hear certain lessons that they could benefit from.

However, the key is still going to be personal effort to invite those who are lost. Those of us who have gotten out of the habit are going to have to get back into that habit. We need to pray about it and work much harder to bring our friends to hear the gospel. Many Christians have almost completely stopped inviting others to our services. We all need to start doing that again.

Let me ask you again, and I want you to give an honest answer. How long has it been since you even tried to get a guest to come to our services? If everyone else put the same amount of effort into bringing outsiders to worship, how many guests would ever come?

"For I am not ashamed of the gospel of Christ, for it is the power of God to salvation for everyone who believes, for the Jew first and also for the Greek" (Romans 1:16).

The gospel still has the power to save souls. But we have to get people there to hear it.

Biblical Insights
August 2002

NOTES

DAY 14

Major Areas of Church Health

When one begins to examine the health and spiritual condition of the local church, seven areas of emphasis need to be evaluated and strengthened. This discussion will provide an overview of these seven areas. Each one of these sections deserves its own full review.

There are two considerations in each of these areas of church life. The most important question is whether what we are doing pleases God. That is, does the Bible teach us to do what we are doing, or have we merely been doing these things because that's the way things have always been done around here?

The second question is whether the methods we have chosen to help us accomplish God's will are the best and most effective ways to do so. In many cases, God has told us what to do, but He has left the how to do it up to us. We need to be "wise as serpents and harmless as doves" in our choice of effective (and scriptural) methods of doing His will.

Worship
We are taught to worship God in "spirit and truth" (John 4:23-24). How we are to worship is outlined in the pages of the New Testament. Worship is to serve two purposes. First and foremost, it is to praise and thank God. Secondly, it is for the building up of one another.

At times, we may need to have some training about worship. We might need to have some singing training to learn how to do that well. There needs to be an emphasis on the Lord's Supper during worship as we recall on a weekly basis what Jesus did for us on the cross. Those who lead in any aspect of our services should be trained in how to do it well. And we must not merely worship based on the teaching of the New Testament, but we must also worship with the right kind of heart (or spirit). Our attitude should be correct before God.

We should examine every aspect of our worship and see if there are ways we can praise Him better (without changing how we worship to please ourselves).

Strengthening the Local Church

Spiritual education and training

We have already written about the benefits of having an organized teaching curriculum for both adults and children. There should also be teacher training by qualified instructors so that we can do the very best job possible of teaching God's word. Special classes outside of our regular curriculum can help fill in some gaps in our Bible knowledge. There should be an intentional closeness among teachers, shepherds, and parents to provide feedback for one another to the spiritual benefit of our young people.

Personal evangelism

Jesus calls His followers to be "fishers of men" (Matthew 4:19). Much of this work is done individually by disciples who seek to help others to become disciples as well. Classes need to be held to equip and train Christians to learn how to teach the lost effectively. We should encourage not only public classes but home Bible studies as well. There must also be follow-up studies to help new Christians grow mature in Christ.

Hospitality

The Lord teaches us to be hospitable to one another (1 Peter 4:9) and to strangers (Hebrews 13:2). Christians should spend time together outside of assemblies as we seek to help one another remain strong in Christ. We should have other disciples over to our homes for parties, singings, and other social activities. We should go on outings together and desire to spend quality time with other Christians in many different settings.

Evangelism efforts

In addition to our individual efforts, there should be church level evangelistic events and opportunities for us to seek and save the lost (Luke 19:10). Gospel meetings, Vacation Bible Schools, and social media should all be utilized to open up doors of opportunity for the lost to learn about the Savior. The church is to be "the pillar and ground of the truth" (1 Timothy 3:15), and we should intentionally plan to provide chances for the lost to attend and learn the truth.

Leadership

The leaders of the local church (shepherds, elders, pastors, overseers, and bishops) should set a good example for others to follow spiritually. They should set the pace for evangelistic work and be personally involved in people's lives to help them become more like Christ and develop strength in areas where they need to grow.

There should be ongoing training for future leaders who can serve God's people as shepherds, rather than waiting until something happens to the current leadership before we begin to think about the future. The importance of leadership cannot be overstated, but far too many churches have underestimated the need to train new leaders.

From the pulpit

The preaching from the pulpit should be balanced to meet the spiritual needs of both new Christians and long-time members. There should be an emphasis on evangelism and a focus on Jesus that reminds us of the One to whom we belong and whom we serve (Acts 27:23).

It is incumbent on the pulpit preaching to raise the level of commitment in the church as a whole. And the preacher must both teach what is right and show the way by example as well.

Conclusion

These seven areas of emphasis are vitally important if we want to be the church that the Lord expects us to be. Some of these things concern our personal obligations to God, while others relate to the collective actions of the congregation.

There is nothing negative about our need to constantly examine our practices to make certain that they are both true to the Bible and effective in accomplishing what God wants us to do. If we need to improve in some areas, let us prayerfully plan to grow in our devotion and dedication to Him.

And let us never forget that we are to do everything to the glory of God (1 Corinthians 10:31).

NOTES

DAY 15

How Involved Are You?

I don't mean, "How is the local church doing?" I mean, "How involved are you personally in the work of the Lord?"

Too many Christians are content to sit back and let others do the behind-the-scenes work in the church. And then, some are quick to criticize and complain that the church just doesn't seem to be getting anywhere. If that is true, how much of that is your fault?

God's design for the church is for every part of the body to be active and working. We learn this all through the New Testament, in passages such as Ephesians 4:11-16, Romans 12, and 1 Corinthians 12.

Are you doing your part?

As you examine your relationship with God (2 Corinthians 13:5) and the things you do for Him as a disciple of Christ, think about how long it has been since you did some of these basic, easy things. When was the last time you...

- Visited a person who is sad and lonely, just to try to cheer them up?

- Told a teenager how proud you are of him (or her) spiritually?

- Invited a non-Christian to services?

- Told someone that you love them? It might be your spouse, your children, your parents, grandparents, aunts, uncles, cousins, or simply friends.

- Sacrificed a personal item you wanted so you could give a little more money to the Lord's work?

- Hugged your children for no real reason?

- Thanked the elders for doing their often thankless job of trying to help us make it to heaven?

Strengthening the Local Church

- Invited another family to come to your home for a Bible study or maybe for a fun evening of food and games?

- Wrote a card of love and encouragement to someone who is hurting for attention and understanding?

- Read through the New Testament in your Bible? (You could easily read the entire New Testament in six months.)

- Wrote a note of appreciation to your adult Bible class teacher or those who teach your children?

- Expressed your appreciation to our great song leaders for the marvelous job they do in leading us in worship?

- Thanked the deacons for their dedicated, mostly behind-the-scenes work?

- Prayed for more laborers to enter the harvest (Matthew 9:37-38)?

- Offered to babysit for a young couple so they could have a date night without their small children?

- Thanked the Lord for the good church where you worship and all the godly people who, although not perfect, are trying with all their hearts to serve the Lord?

Have you ever heard the phrase, "If it is to be, it is up to me?" That could easily be the motto of every disciple of Christ. If we would all take the personal initiative to do what we can in the Lord's service, this world would be a much better place in which to live. And more souls would be saved for eternity in heaven.

Here is a list of things all Christians can do without being asked or told:
1. Send a card to the sick, lonely, or bereaved.
2. Visit the sick, lonely, or shut-in.
3. Visit new members; have them into your home.
4. Visit the absentees and encourage them.
5. Worship regularly with the saints and be on time for services.
6. Contribute regularly to the reverence of the assembly.
7. Read and study your Bible and pray every day.
8. Distribute some good literature to a lost person.
9. Use your car to bring others to services.

10. Take flowers to the sick and shut-ins.
11. Teach home Bible classes or arrange them in your home.
12. Be friendly and greet guests to the services.
13. Develop hospitality among one another.
14. Give as God has prospered you.
15. Use your telephone in contacting and encouraging others.
16. Take food to the sick, needy, and bereaved.
17. Live godly and peaceful lives.
18. Pray for one another, especially the elders, preachers, and teachers.
19. Participate in all phases of church activities.
20. Lend a helping hand.

Here is something to think about. "If you cannot do great things, do small things in a great way." I have heard that for years, and when I looked it up on the internet, it was attributed to a man named Napoleon Hill. I don't know who he is, but I do like what he said. Consider how you can apply that saying to your own life.

"Therefore, my beloved brothers, be steadfast, immovable, always abounding in the work of the Lord, knowing that in the LORD your labor is not in vain" (1 Corinthians 15:58, ESV). Did you catch that word, abounding? Could your work for the Lord be described as abounding? Or is it lacking? Or missing entirely? Could you do more?

What are you personally doing to help the local church grow, both numerically and spiritually?

NOTES

DAY 16

The Core Values

This article pertains to some of the core values of who and what God wants us to be as His people. These are vital Biblical doctrines that must be maintained and that cannot be compromised. What are some of these distinguishing teachings that separate the Lord's church from man-made denominations? What are some of the Biblical truths that we must always cling to, no matter what else happens to us or around us?

In Proverbs 22:28, the phrase "ancient landmark" refers to property boundaries (usually a large stone that marks the end of one person's property and the beginning of their neighbor's land) – see also Proverbs 23:10-11. The Law of Moses prohibited moving these landmarks (Deuteronomy 19:14; 27:17). This was a matter of honesty and integrity.

A similar thought is found in Jeremiah 6:16, where the spiritual landmarks that God had set in place, and which should never be moved, are referred to as "the old paths."

While our methods may change with time, and how we present these ideas to people may vary, the truth of the gospel must never be compromised.

1) Undenominational Christianity
   There is only one true church; it is the one Jesus promised to build in Matthew 16:18. Christ is the one head of the one body (Colossians 1:18). Further study of the New Testament shows us that each local church (sometimes we use the term, congregation or assembly) is autonomous, that is, independent and self-governing.

   The overseers (or elders) are appointed to watch out for the souls of the members, and they are the only authority over a local church (1 Peter 5:1-4). They serve under the authority of Jesus in heaven.

   The Lord's church is not one denomination among many. It is undenominational. We are not trying to be the best denomination. As a matter of fact, we are not trying to be a denomination at all. We are just trying to be the church you can read about on the pages of the New Testament. There were no denominations in the first century.

2) Who is a Christian?
We must never underestimate the value of God's plan of salvation, as outlined in the New Testament. We must stand firmly for the truth that one must believe in Christ as God's Son (this is sometimes called faith), that we must repent or turn our hearts and lives away from sin, and we must be baptized in the name of Christ for the remission of sins. Mark 16:15-16; Acts 2:38; and Acts 22:16 are just a few passages among many that teach us how to be saved.

Infant baptism, salvation by faith only, and once saved, always saved are doctrines of men, not of God. People who believe these things are not saved because they have not done what the Bible tells us to do to be forgiven of our sins. I am not trying to be mean or hateful about that; I am just trying to show what the Bible teaches. If we don't really think lost people are lost, we won't try to save them.

3) True Worship
This includes the Lord's Supper every first day of the week and no instrumental music, which are two areas where many denominations have abandoned God's word. New Testament worship is not fancy, and it is not entertainment. It is a reverent celebration of all that God has done for us (1 Corinthians 14:40). It is directed to God and must please Him. He has told us in the Bible what He wants us to do in worship. We cannot compromise with anyone to change what He has said.

4) Bible authority
"And whatever you do in word or deed, do all in the name of the Lord Jesus, giving thanks to God the Father through Him" (Colossians 3:17). That means we only do what He has told us to do in every area of our service.

"If anyone speaks, let him speak as the oracles of God..." (1 Peter 4:11). This passage is the basis for the statement that "we speak where the Bible speaks and are silent where the Bible is silent."

The whole question of the silence of the scriptures deserves a lot of study and meditation.

5) The difference between the Old Testament and the New Testament
   Many people turn back to the Old Testament for authority for their actions. It is vital that we understand that the Old Law was "nailed to the cross" and replaced with the New Testament (Colossians 2:14). That is why we don't offer animal sacrifices, why we don't worship on the Sabbath Day (which is Saturday), why we don't use instruments of music, and many other things.

6) The work of the church
   The work of the church is spiritual, not social. "But if I am delayed, I write so that you may know how you ought to conduct yourself in the house of God, which is the church of the living God, the pillar and ground of the truth" (1 Timothy 3:15).

   We must have an over-riding confidence that the power of the gospel will convict, convert, and transform our world.

   Many people don't understand this. Churches around the world have increasingly turned to secular appeals to get people to attend. And those who offer the most social activities often have the biggest crowds. But it is the gospel that will save people, not social and recreational events.

7) The importance of unity
   Everyone in the church needs to be on the same page and working together under the authority of the New Testament. Ephesians 4:1-3, 4-6, and 16 emphasize unity and the need for every part of the body to do his or her share of the work.

Conclusion
Why are these things important? Because they all come from the Bible.

Please understand that I am not trying to create a creed consisting of seven items that all "faithful" churches must accept to meet God's approval. This is simply an attempt to emphasize some of the Biblical principles of New Testament Christianity that seem important to me as I read the scriptures.

Remember that these are non-negotiable truths. And there are others; these just stand out to me as being the difference between the true faith that comes from heaven and a false hope that originates with men.

NOTES

DAY 17

The Value of Vacation Bible School

Some of my fondest childhood memories include attending Vacation Bible School at various congregations in the Southern Illinois community where I grew up.

The church where my family attended started conducting a VBS early in my lifetime. It was always a highlight of my young summers, and I enjoyed it so much that I usually went to 3 or 4 different VBS series at different congregations each year.

I most clearly remember a wall chart that one of our elders used to help us learn the books of the Bible, both Old Testament and New Testament. He made it on a huge sheet that covered a big part of one wall of the auditorium. It was popular in those days, before projectors and PowerPoint, to use bed sheets with charts drawn on them in gospel meetings and other teaching settings. Gospel meetings would often consist of a single chart on a bed sheet discussing various subjects or book studies from the Bible, and the preacher would use that chart every night. At VBS, we learned the divisions about the testaments: Old Testament, which includes Law, History, Poetry, Major Prophets and Minor Prophets, and New Testament, which includes Gospels, History (Acts), Epistles (or letters), and Prophecy (Revelation). And then we would all say the books in order every day.

I recall a time when attending another congregation's VBS and having the lady who taught my class say to me, "Wow, you can really find those verses in your Bible. You are the fastest one in the class." Do you think that made me feel good? Of course it did, and I remember it more than fifty years later.

Tremendous value to the local church can be seen in conducting a Vacation Bible School. Our desire is to teach the Bible to as many people as possible, right? In my experience, as a child, an adult, and a preacher, more guests are willing to attend a VBS than almost any other special event.

If the congregation where you worship doesn't have a VBS (maybe you used to have one but haven't in the last several years), it might be a really good teaching opportunity that can reach some lost souls for the Lord.

In 2017, I had the privilege to preach regularly for a church that was between preachers. Early in the year, someone mentioned that they were disappointed that they didn't have very many children. A lot of churches are like that, and it is a very difficult trend to reverse. Young families with small children are drawn to churches that have other children to be friends with their children. So if there are only a few young ones, many families decide to worship where there are more kids. It can be a self-defeating cycle.

I asked why they quit having VBS because I knew they had previously enjoyed good crowds at VBS. They told me that they didn't think they had enough children to have a Vacation Bible School. But it seems to me that this is exactly why it would be helpful to have one. If you don't have VBS and it would attract others to the church, why not try having one? It will be small at first, but if you have faith that God's word will not return to Him void, then it is worth the effort. If you have four children and they each bring a friend, you have planted seeds of God's truth in the hearts and minds of eight young people.

That church had seven children in Bible class on Sunday before we held a one-day VBS on Saturday. We had forty one children and forty adults attend classes that day. Everyone was thrilled, of course, and we repeated the effort in 2018 with similar results.

There are lots of ways to conduct a Vacation Bible Study. Many churches have a five-day study – Monday through Friday, either in the day time or the evening. A recent trend has been to have these special classes for children for over three days, from Sunday through Tuesday. We tried an idea that I had read about several years ago from a church in Indiana that had a one-day Saturday study. We chose that plan to start with and began at 9:30 and ended at about 2:30 in the afternoon. Individuals paid for a lunch break at a local pizza shop, and then we came back for more classes and songs.

Our theme was Faith, Hope, and Love, three classes with three separate Bible stories. We wrote our own class material. It was marvelous, and the children had a wonderful time. The church members really worked very hard to invite people to the class and to prepare and deliver the lessons.

After the first two years, the elders decided that, due to a number of very small children who needed to take a nap in the early afternoon, they would shorten the one-day study to last from 9:30 to noon. Since then, we have had two Bible study lessons, and in between, lots of songs and Bible drills. It still makes for a wonderful and impactful day in these children's lives. They love it and so do the adults.

The biggest benefit from VBS is that it shows our young people how important they are to the church and, therefore, to the Lord. It helps children become excited about learning the Bible, and that is always good.

It is also helpful for adults as well. Churches that have VBS in the evening usually have better attendance, and teachers who volunteer are able to do so, even if they work during the day, so you have a bigger pool of workers.

Songs are a really important part of a VBS. The children always enjoy them, plus you can teach them important things through song. Songs may make it easier for them to memorize the days of creation, the sons of Jacob, the judges, the books of the Old and New Testaments, and lots of other valuable things.

Remember that you are planting seeds of truth in young hearts. What was it that brought the prodigal son to his senses in Christ's parable (Luke 15:11-32)? It was what he had been taught when he lived at home with his father. He had rebelled against that for a while (haven't a lot of our young people in the church made this same tragic choice?), but he was brought back by what he remembered from his youth.

A Vacation Bible School does not have to be "big" to be a success or to have an eternal impact on souls. If you have ten children and show them that they matter to the Lord, it can make a difference in eternity. The number is not the important issue. If you have two or three children, make this a special event that they will remember forever.

But if you aren't going to work hard to prepare useful and practical Bible lessons, if you aren't going to make much effort to invite friends, neighbors, family members, if you don't really want it to succeed, don't waste your time and effort. If it is worth doing, it is worth doing right.

If you are willing to really work at this, VBS can be a powerful teaching opportunity for the people of God. Do it right, and you will reap eternal rewards that will honor and glorify God and save souls.

NOTES

DAY 18

Some Important Leadership Principles

There are a number of essentials when it comes to having a growing church. One of the most important factors is having a sense of direction that comes from leadership in tune with God's word and the needs of a lost world. I want to discuss three vital principles about the needs of a church that will grow and prosper in a hostile world.

These leadership principles must be present in a church that wants to grow. God's plan is that leadership be provided in a local church by scripturally qualified shepherds who lead and guide the people toward heaven. Many churches do not have elders who can lead the church in that way, but even if there are no "official" leaders, someone must keep the church on track in following God's will. If there are no elders, someone must point the church in the right direction. Often, this task falls to the preacher, so here are some things I hope will help.

1) Forward thinking

   Far too many churches worship their past and continue to cling to outdated ideas and methods to reach the lost. Just because a Bible correspondence course had 400 students and the church baptized fifty of them back in the 1960s doesn't necessarily mean it will still work today. (I am not against using correspondence studies; if they are up to date in appearance and challenging in content, they can still work. But we often use old-fashioned looking stuff today to save money in a world where we can do much better with little expense.)

   Paul said, in Philippians 3:12-14, that he would press on in his service to God, without being bound by his past. (Whether you think he meant his past failures or his past successes doesn't matter; he was going to keep moving forward from that point onward.)

   Decisions need to be made regarding Bible classes, budgets, buildings, and other matters that should be geared toward helping people reach heaven. We should not simply be interested in keeping house or just holding our own (while we wait until we have elders).

Two questions should drive our decision making-process. First, is it scriptural? Second, will it help people go to heaven?

2) Focus on really important matters

In Matthew 6:33, the Savior reminds us not to think too much or to worry about the things of this world, including material possessions. Rather, He says, "But seek first the kingdom of God and His righteousness, and all these things (physical needs, rh) shall be added to you."

The Lord is not saying that we don't need to take care of ourselves physically, but He is emphasizing that we must learn to put first things first. Some things are just more important to God than other things, and we should learn which is which and have those same priorities.

I don't know who said it first, but a lot of people have repeated it, and I think it certainly has value for us today. "The main thing is keeping the main thing the main thing." Doesn't that make sense?

There are some really important goals we need to accomplish. We need to help people become Christians. We need to help new Christians grow spiritually. We need to help the weak grow stronger. We need to help the fallen return.

In the final analysis, it is all about souls and saving them to the glory of God.

The devil will make certain that there will be many distractions, anything that can derail us or cause us to procrastinate from doing the right thing.

- Some people will get sick physically.
- Someone will hurt your feelings.
- Not everyone will do the right thing.
- You will study the Bible with people who do not obey.
- Some Christians will just quit.
- Temptations will grow stronger and more frequent.

But in the midst of all of these difficulties, the ship must stay the course. That's really the point of Luke 9:57-62. It shows us how important serving Christ is, and we must never give up.

3) A deep sense of dependence on God

"I am the vine, you are the branches. He who abides in Me, and I in him, bears much fruit; for without Me you can do nothing" (John 15:5).

"I can do all things through Christ who strengthens me" (Philippians 4:13).

We are dependent on Him for everything we do. He is the One who saves souls (1 Corinthians 3:6); we are simply seed spreaders. He is the one who builds up Christians (Philippians 1:6); we are merely the vessels He works with and through.

We must emphasize prayer to God in all we do as we pray for ourselves and for others.

If we try to do things by our own strength, in our own way, for our glory, with human ideas, we will fail.

It is not about us. It is all about Him. It is all for Him.

Conclusion

Those who lead in a local church need to remember these principles when making the decisions.

God's plan is for elders and deacons, and every church needs to work to have that scriptural organization. Even then, the shepherds should continue to use these divine principles to guide us to heaven.

Until then, these ideals and values can be used to help the church prosper and please God.

Strengthening the Local Church

NOTES

Strengthening the Local Church

DAY 19

The Importance of Worship

There are many things in life that, if we are not careful, we can begin to take for granted and just ignore any opportunity for improvement. Worship is one of those things. We can grow accustomed to doing the same things week after week, to the point where we go through the motions without the appropriate thoughtfulness that should go into what we offer to our God. Worship, after all, is designed to honor Him, not to make us happy or fulfilled.

Our worship services should be plain and straightforward, as described in the New Testament, yet also powerful in expressing our gratitude to God for all His blessings and uplifting for us as we participate in heartfelt praise of the Creator.

While we direct our worship to God, we must also be aware of the impact it can or will have on the guests who attend our assemblies. While the main point in 1 Corinthians 14 is how those early Christians were using or abusing their spiritual gifts, Paul also emphasizes that non-Christians who come to our services need to understand what we are doing and why (verses 15-16, 22-25). When they are present, they need to feel and understand that "God is truly among you" (verse 25). If they leave without feeling that they have been in God's presence, then we have not really worshiped properly.

(We must be careful not to conduct our worship services to impress visitors, however. That's why so many religious groups have turned to entertainment and mere performances. But it is true that they should be impressed with the reverence and devotion that our services demonstrate. What we do in worship should touch their hearts, not merely their funny bones.)

So let's think for a while about the importance of our worship. Anything we do for God should be of utmost importance to us. We should take it very seriously and seek to do God's work in God's ways. Doesn't that make sense? What does the New Testament tell us about our worship?

Strengthening the Local Church

The word "worship" in English comes from the idea of worth or value. We are expressing to God, His worth-ship, an acknowledgment of His greatness and majesty, along with our submission to His will. Two basic Greek words in the New Testament are translated as worship (actually, there are five; two of them are prominent). One refers to bowing down toward (not necessarily physically, although there are several places in scripture where that is exactly what is meant). The other speaks of serving, giving religious service to or for.

One of the key passages about worship is found within the context of an interaction between Jesus and a sinful Samaritan woman in John 4. Jesus and the disciples are traveling from Judea to Galilee (verse 2) and are passing through Samaria (to the north of Judea and to the south of Galilee). As they come to a city called Sychar, Jesus pauses to rest and sits by a water well while His followers go into town to buy some food. As the time approaches noon, a woman from the city comes to the well to draw water, and Jesus asks her for a drink. This request begins a conversation that quickly turns to spiritual matters.

Jesus tells her about living water. He asks to talk with her husband, and she realizes, when He knows so much about her and her past, that He is no ordinary man. She believes Him to be a prophet and asks Him about the proper place to worship (verse 20). Should worship be conducted on Mount Gerizim as the Samaritans did , or is Jerusalem (Mount Zion) the better place? Jesus responds with these words: "Woman, believe Me, the hour is coming when you will neither on this mountain, nor in Jerusalem, worship the Father. You worship what you do not know; we know what we worship, for salvation is of the Jews. But the hour is coming, and now is, when the true worshipers will worship the Father in spirit and truth; for the Father is seeking such to worship Him. God is Spirit, and those who worship Him must worship in spirit and truth" (verses 21-24).

Jesus quickly lets her (and us) know that worship is not limited to any single location but may be found wherever people seek the Father. He also informs her that there is such a thing as "true" worship, which implies that there is also false worship. Some worship pleases God; some forms of so-called worship do not. There are two aspects of true worship, according to God's Son, spirit and truth.

The character of worship that pleases God is in the phrase, "in spirit." Spiritual worship comes from a heart in a proper relationship with God. Your heart and attitude must be right, not only toward God, but also with each other (see Matthew 5:23-24). This character of worship is one of the reasons why Christians are referred to as "a royal priesthood" (1 Peter 2:5, 9-10), so that we may offer our whole lives and hearts to the God of heaven.

Worship in spirit, then, tells us that there must be a balance between celebration and reverence. Our attitude must be one of gratitude for all of the gifts and blessings that the Creator has bestowed on His creation. We are to celebrate what He has done for us. There must also be a sense of awe and respect for God. It is true that we should enjoy worship, but it is not a pep rally (1 Corinthians 14:40). We are in the presence of the God of the universe and should reflect our submission to Him (see Exodus 3:4-6 and 20:18; Psalm 111:9; Hebrews 12:28-29).

But worship services are not comparable to a funeral service. It is alright to smile and even to laugh out loud at times because we enjoy thanking God and lifting our praises to Him. (You can see this attitude in the book of Psalms; ten of them are called "Hallelujah Psalms" (106, 111-13, 135, 146-150). Hallelujah means "praise the Lord," and we should not be afraid of that phrase or idea.

The second quality of worship is the standard, or what we ought to do in worship, "in truth." We should offer all things to God according to what Jesus taught His disciples about worship and what we read about the early church doing in worship under the leadership of His inspired apostles and prophets. Worship means we are doing what God wants, not what we want or like.

So is your personal worship toward God meaningful or empty? Do you really focus on what you are saying and doing, or do you just go through the motions without any heartfelt devotion? When you sing, do you do so with reverence for God (Ephesians 5:19) and pay attention to the words? When you partake of the Lord's Supper, do you think about the body and blood of Jesus every time and really examine your heart? When you give, do you do so from a willing, sacrificial heart? When you listen to a lesson from the word of God, do you think about personal application to improve your life and service to Him? When you pray (or listen to the prayer leader), do you really worship God?

God's people have often struggled with growing bored with God's plan. For a couple of examples, read Malachi 1:6-14 and 1 Corinthians 11:20-32.

Strengthening the Local Church

In an attempt to make worship more exciting, people have done some unbelievable things, such as dimming the lights, adding instrumental music, choirs, and rock bands, as well as drama productions and plays. They have also limited the repertoire to fast, peppy songs, encouraging swaying and clapping to the music. The common ingredient is that these are all external things, while true worship comes from within. Christianity is not half-hearted service, but whole-hearted sacrifice. Our worship should reflect the joy and gratitude of our hearts for God and all that He has done for us.

NOTES

DAY 20

Improving Our Assemblies

If we don't pay enough attention to what we do when we come together for worship and Bible study assemblies, they can gradually (although unintentionally) slip in their quality.

We need to remember, as yesterday's emphasis on worship stated, that we are to assemble to the glory of God. Assemblies of God's people are primarily opportunities to thank Him and praise Him for all that He has done and continues to do for us.

But assemblies also have the secondary purpose of helping to strengthen and build up His people. For example, our songs, while mostly about praising God, also serve to edify us as disciples. "Let the word of Christ dwell in you richly in all wisdom, teaching and admonishing one another in psalms and hymns and spiritual songs, singing with grace in your hearts to the Lord" (Colossians 3:16). That verse mentions both "singing with grace in your hearts to the Lord" (worship) and "teaching and admonishing one another" (edification). Much of what we do when we assemble contains both aspects.

There is one more aspect to mention, just briefly, about our services. That is the impression that our assemblies can have on non-Christians. While not as significant as the other two, we need to think about this part of our worship as well.

One of the parts of our assemblies that has a major impact on our guests is our singing. If the singing is really good, it can leave a very positive impression on their minds. However, if the singing is bad, it can leave a negative impression in their minds and perhaps cause them to not return. Sometimes we can't do anything about that, but if we can improve what we do when we come together, we should try to do so, for God. There are quite a few really excellent song leaders in the brotherhood and some of them conduct singing and song leader training classes to help improve this aspect of congregational worship. It might be worthwhile to bring in some talented people to conduct classes like that in the local church. People who know music can try to teach it to others who would appreciate the help.

Strengthening the Local Church

Christians can also get together in homes on occasion to learn some new songs and how to sing them well. Those interested in improving worship can listen to CDs or download available songs from the internet to teach them to members.

Please realize that we are talking about having more powerful, God-exalting worship, not better and more professional entertainment. There is a difference.

Many passages in the New Testament that speak to our public assemblies, but let's focus on the one in Hebrews 10:23-25: "Let us hold fast the confession of our hope without wavering, for He who promised is faithful. And let us consider one another to stir up love and good works, not forsaking the assembling of ourselves together, as is the manner of some, but exhorting one another, and so much the more as you see the Day approaching." There are five verbs (action words) in those verses that tell us how to make our assemblies more profitable spiritually.

1. Hold Fast
   This means to hold onto something firmly and not let it go. Many in the first century were turning back to Judaism, and some to the world. That's really why the book of Hebrews was written: to encourage these first-century disciples to remain faithful to God. Notice in verses 35-39 that the unknown author of the book tells them not to give up personally, even if others around them were doing so. In Chapter 11, he will give them one example after another of the personal faith of many Old Testament people, both men and women, who persevered and remained true to God in very difficult circumstances. The writer is saying to them, "They held on; so can you." The Hebrew writer adds the phrase, "without wavering." That refers to being consistently faithful, not on again, off again in our faith.

2. Consider one another
   The word "consider" means to perceive clearly. The author of Hebrews is talking about thoughtfully looking for ways and opportunities to help each other (Philippians 2:4). Our assemblies give us the chance to not simply think about "what can I get out of worship/class," but "how can I help someone else to grow?" He wants us to think about, realize, and be considerate of how our words and actions affect others (Colossians 3:12-14). If other disciples were to imitate your example, would the local church be stronger or weaker? Be honest here. Your influence on others can be considerable; we need to make certain we are setting a positive example for others, not a negative one.

Improving Our Assemblies

3. Stir up love and good works

    "Stir up" means to stimulate. And what we are to encourage in other believers is "love and good works." The NIV translates this phrase as "let us consider how we may spur one another on toward love and good deeds." Again, the idea here is to have a positive influence on others. If they see us doing good things, they may well be prompted to do good things also. Proverbs 27:17 describes this idea as iron sharpening iron. Do not forget that one of the purposes of our assemblies is to remind us of our duties to God. This is called "edification" (Romans 14:19). It is one of the reasons Christ established the church in the first place, as a kind of mutual edification society where we are supposed to build each other up spiritually.

4. Not forsaking the assembling together.

    The fourth verb here is stated negatively, do not forsake the assembling together. Stated in a positive way, he is telling us to be faithful and regular in our attendance. He warns that this was becoming "the manner" of some. Other versions translate this as habit or custom. It is easy to get into the habit of missing here and there, until people sometimes just quit coming altogether. We can probably all think of people who used to attend all the time, but they have long ago quit coming. If some people showed up at their job with the kind of irregularity they show toward church attendance, they would have already been fired. Earlier in Hebrews 5:12-14, the writer warns about those who are not growing as they should. You cannot grow if you don't attend, and you cannot help others to grow either if you aren't there. That's why schools have a strict attendance policy, because students can't learn what they aren't there to hear from the teacher. The same principle applies to the spiritual realm.

5. Exhorting one another.

    Most of the newer translations use the word "encouraging" one another. Much of what the Hebrew writer is emphasizing here falls into the category of our influence on others. Use this time together to help each other learn how to serve God better. It is to be an encouraging time together. (At times rebuke is needed, but even that is to be done in love; a better way is to encourage them to do right, rather than criticizing them for doing wrong.) Make helpful comments in Bible class. Participate in the song service. Speak to others before and after services. Use this time to get to know others you may not know very well (especially if there are those who don't seem to get much attention). Help young mothers with children and no husband there to help. Show warmth and friendliness. Treat others like friends and show them the love of God. Emphasize being happy to be together as a family.

Use the time we have with other Christians wisely and build each other up in the Lord.

NOTES

DAY 21

Rescue the Perishing

Throughout the world, there are literally thousands of former Christians who are "out of service" to the Lord. Back in the late 1970s or early 1980s, I remember reading an article by Leslie Diestelkamp in a paper called "Think," in which he stated that there were an estimated 30,000 unfaithful members in the Chicago area where he was living at that time. (I tried to find the exact date of the article, but I couldn't put my hands on it.) Do you think the situation has gotten better or worse since then? In that same article, he mentioned that there was a congregation in Wisconsin with fifty members, but they were aware of 200-300 former members still in the area. (I am certainly not picking on Chicago or Wisconsin, and neither was brother Diestelkamp.) These kinds of numbers are probably true everywhere else also.

The point is simply to say that we have a lot of work to do, and we're just trying to see if we can go out and do our best to bring some of those lost souls back to God. We should not forget about our brothers and sisters who have made mistakes (we have made some too, maybe just different ones) and act like we don't care about them because they made some wrong choices.

Do you remember the parable of the lost sheep, where the shepherd had 100 sheep and one of them wandered away? He searched diligently and tirelessly until he found it and rejoiced greatly when the sheep was safely back home (Luke 15:1-7).

Do you remember the next parable in Luke 15:8-10, where a woman had 10 silver coins and lost one of them? She worked faithfully, sweeping her house until she recovered what was lost? Again, there was a lot of rejoicing between her and her neighbors.

Those parables and the one about the two lost sons that follows (verses 11-32) are all about how much lost souls matter to God. Jesus tells us that there is "joy in the presence of the angels of God over one sinner who repents." The father of the prodigal son (who represents God in this parable) threw a huge party to celebrate the return of his wayward son. God wants all His children to come back to Him.

Strengthening the Local Church

We (by that, I mean Christians who are still trying to serve God) have lost a lot of people we care about in the last many years. Young people are leaving the Lord in record numbers. Older people are passing away. Many churches are not even "holding their own" when it comes to members, let alone growing and bringing in new members. With the help of our Almighty God, we must reverse this trend.

Maybe one of the first things we need to do (led by the elders if the church where you worship has them) is make a list of people we know who live in the area where the church is located, who used to be members of the Lord's church but who no longer faithfully attend services. Don't they deserve some of our attention so we can try to bring them back before it is eternally too late? God hasn't quit loving them and wanting what is best for them, and we must not forget about them either.

Here is a letter I wrote several years ago to an unfaithful Christian. Maybe this letter will give you some things to think about as you consider trying to restore some brother or sister who has left the Lord.

> Dear Friend,
>
> I don't know if you will remember me or not. I am a member of the church of Christ that you attended some time ago. I was reading the Bible the other day and came across a passage that encouraged me to write you. It was in Galatians 6:1-2. "Brethren, if a man is overtaken in any trespass, you who are spiritual restore such a one in a spirit of gentleness, considering yourself lest you also be tempted. Bear one another's burdens, and so fulfill the law of Christ." I thought about you when I read those verses. So you see, the Lord asked me to contact you. I want to help bear your burden.
>
> I don't really know why you left the church. Perhaps you got discouraged somehow. Maybe somebody said something unkind to you. Maybe a friend encouraged you to do something wrong, and you didn't feel like facing your brothers and sisters. It really doesn't matter why; it just matters that you became unfaithful.
>
> Perhaps you do not realize the consequences of your situation. You have given up something more valuable and

precious than anything else in the entire world, the hope of eternal life. Jesus Christ died for your sins. You knew that. You obeyed the truth. Your sins were forgiven. But then you became unfaithful and left the Lord. The Bible describes your situation in this way. "For if, after they have escaped the pollutions of the world through the knowledge of the Lord and Savior Jesus Christ, they are again entangled in them and overcome, the latter end is worse for them than the beginning" (2 Peter 2:20).

I am afraid you have forgotten the seriousness of obedience and the obligations you have to God. The Bible teaches that a Christian has not made a shallow step in his or her life, but actually has made a lifetime, total commitment. See Revelation 2:10, 1 Corinthians 15:58, Matthew 24:13.

The value of your soul (Matthew 16:26), the horrible punishment of hell (Mark 9:43-44), and the wonderful reward of heaven (Revelation 21:4) are all things which should encourage you to return to the fold of safety.

You must repent of your unfaithfulness to the Lord (Acts 8:22), confess your faults (James 5:16), and we will pray for you. You can be restored to faithful service, and we would love to have you back. Please, think about it seriously. Don't you want to go to heaven? I hope you do! Why not return? Please...

Conclusion

I hope some of those thoughts might help you remember to do what you can in this area. You probably know some people who have given up. Let's see what we can do to restore their hope of heaven.

The old song, Rescue the Perishing, reminds us of our responsibility in this area:

Rescue the perishing, Care for the dying,
Snatch them in pity from sin and the grave;
Weep o'er the erring one, Lift up the fallen,
Tell them of Jesus, the mighty to save.

Strengthening the Local Church

Rescue the perishing, Duty demands it;
Strength for thy labor the Lord will provide:
Back to the narrow way, Patiently win them;
Tell the poor wanderer a Savior has died.

Chorus
Rescue the perishing, Care for the dying;
Jesus is merciful, Jesus will save.

NOTES

_____
_____
_____
_____
_____
_____
_____
_____
_____
_____
_____
_____
_____
_____
_____
_____
_____
_____
_____

DAY 22

Navigating Changes

We have talked a lot in these pages about things that may well need to be changed in the local church where you worship (maybe not, but some churches will need more work than others). However, some people really hate any change at all, and so improving what we do is often easier said than done.

Many sincere Christians are reluctant to change anything because they mistakenly equate all change with doctrinal compromise. I hope you will believe that I am not encouraging anyone to change anything God says. However, our human traditions and the way we do what God says can often be changed without violating what the New Testament teaches. We are not suggesting that anyone change the gospel message, the organization of the church, or the worship of the church. Those things are set in stone, that is, they are determined by God and not up to us to change. But the order of our worship, the number of songs we sing, what time we meet, or how many times per week we meet, are all things that we can vary without displeasing God. By making some of those changes, churches can make things better. We must strive for excellence in all we do for God so that He is glorified by everything we do for Him.

I have two major suggestions when it comes to change in the local church. First, do not try to change too much too fast. That will scare people. Preach about it, talk outside of services about it, pray about it, preach about it again, and then maybe do it or maybe wait a little longer. (You have heard the old joke about how to eat an elephant? One bite at a time.) If you ram through a whole bunch of changes all at once, you are only asking for trouble.

Second, and it actually was mentioned already, do not change anything without prayer. I have had lots of ideas that I thought were great, but after considering them carefully and praying about them, they didn't seem so awesome. If I had pushed those ideas on others, often against their will, just because I was excited and thought them to be the right thing to do, it would have been a big mistake. So, be sure to move slowly. Some situations in local churches have taken decades to develop.

Strengthening the Local Church

You should not rush in like a bull in a china shop and start tearing up stuff that has a lot of love and nostalgia behind it.

However, despite our best intentions, some things may very well need to be different. And no matter how long we have been doing something, if it is no longer accomplishing what it used to, change may be the best option and the one that would please God, rather than continuing to exhaust time, money, effort, and goodwill on spinning our wheels. Not all activity is not productive, and we could do lots of things better.

It is vital, as alluded to above, to make certain that the end result of our changes pleases God. Is it something we should be doing at all? Churches should make those decisions through a thorough study of the Bible. We can figure out ways to draw larger crowds, increase our contributions, and make a bigger splash in the community, but many of those ways will not be scriptural. We must never confuse effectiveness with biblical correctness; some times they overlap, but some times they conflict with each other. Here we have to trust God to know what is best for us to do, but we may have some leeway in how we do it. Behind everything we decide, we should ask ourselves, Is it from heaven or from men (Matthew 21:23-27)? Bible study and prayer can help us to determine the difference.

The purpose of all our changes must be to reach more souls with the gospel and save some of them. We will never save everyone we hope to, but there are people out there with good hearts who genuinely want to please God (Luke 8:8, 15). They are not always easy to find, but we need to keep searching. We must not "grow weary while doing good, for in due season we shall reap if we do not lose heart" (Galatians 6:9).

Many of the ideas in this *40 Day Journey to Church Revival* focus on improving ourselves, both individually and collectively. We discuss ways to improve our assemblies, singing, Bible classes, and ourselves as disciples of our Master. Some changes might make us weaker; we want to make changes that will make us better and stronger.

Work on one big thing at a time. Get together and discuss things; brainstorming is always a good idea because it brings together many points of view and ideas so that we hopefully have the best options to consider.

Think about the teaching program for example. What can we do to make the Bible more interesting and valuable to young or old minds?

How can we make applications of the spiritual principles that we read in the Bible? Are there related activities we could do to drive the lessons into the students' minds? Should we change the type of class material we use? Should we write our own? Should we take advantage of all the options available instead of just sticking with something we have always used?

What about appointing elders and deacons? This change should be preceded by a study, discussion, and sermons on the subject to look at the qualifications and duties of those who might be ready to serve. We should be reminded of the responsibilities that those of us who will not be elders have to those who are going to serve the Lord that way. It is a two-way street, and we need to understand our place in the whole arrangement.

When you are talking about how we can reach more lost souls, is there an effective strategy, as well as easy-to-teach material, that we will want to focus on? Do we all need to use the same approach? Can we all do what we want as long as we are teaching the gospel to the lost? What will we do for follow-up material as we strengthen and develop those who are converted? If what the church has been doing hasn't been very effective, how can we do better? How can we save more souls? How can we reach the families, neighbors, friends, classmates, and co-workers of our members?

You can make small changes in the right direction from time to time, but even then, don't try to make too many at the same time. Prepare people for change, and they will be more comfortable with it when those changes are ultimately made.

It is possible, and we must not forget this, that we are doing some things that are not scriptural and therefore, they need to be changed. We should always be willing to examine our current practices in light of the teachings of the New Testament. If we find that something we have done for a long time is not biblical, we must be willing to change. "We've always done it that way" is not the same as "This is what the Bible says." Such changes can be very hard to make, but honesty with God demands that we consider everything.

I recently read a book titled *How to Change Your Church for Good*. Remember that this is what we are talking about here, not change just for the sake of change, but to improve how we do what God wants us to do as His church.

Strengthening the Local Church

One more time, because it cannot be emphasized too much, be sure to pray fervently when introducing new ideas and new ways of doing old things. Jesus said that He will be with us, even to the end of the age (Matthew 28:20). We will never succeed in anything without the Lord's blessings.

NOTES

DAY 23

Racially Integrated Churches

Like many (and I hope, most and I wish, all) Christians, I am bothered by the racial tension in America. It is a shame that, in a highly educated and cultured society like the United States, there is still racial prejudice. Such a situation should never exist, especially in a country claiming to believe that "all men are created equal."

And, in some churches, racial prejudice still exists. Even if it were understandable that such attitudes still abound in the secular world (which it is not), it is inexcusable among those who claim to be God's people.

The Bible speaks of racial prejudice, although not by that name. And, in every case, it is condemned.

In Genesis 43:32, it is said that "the Egyptians could not eat food with the Hebrews, for that is an abomination to the Egyptians."

In Numbers 12, Miriam and Aaron spoke against Moses because "he had married an Ethiopian woman."

In John 4, Jesus Himself encountered a Samaritan woman. The Samaritans were a mixed race of Jew and Gentile. The Jews considered all Gentiles to be unclean. The woman was shocked when Christ asked her for a drink of water (John 4:9). She was surprised for two reasons: she was a woman and she was a Samaritan. Jesus took advantage of the opportunity to tear down some of the walls of prejudice that had existed for years. Race, color, and nationality make no difference to God and should not matter to us.

This Jew and Gentile hatred went back for many years to the time when God sent Israel into captivity in Assyria and the Assyrians repopulated the land with foreigners who then intermarried and created the Samaritan race (see 2 Kings 17:24-41). Jesus broke down that wall between the races (all races) when He died on the cross (see Ephesians 2:11-18).

But in the first century, even strong and faithful Christians would often revert to some of these sinful attitudes. Paul rebuked the apostle Peter for acting sinfully around Christians who were former Gentiles. Paul said that Peter was a hypocrite, was to be blamed, was not straightforward about the truth of the gospel, and that his hypocrisy caused others to sin also (see Galatians 2:11-14). Peter knew better, but he sinned, and it was a clear-cut case of racial prejudice.

It was Peter who had received a three-fold vision from God telling him that God had cleansed all people (and foods) and would no longer accept such prejudice. The gospel had not yet gone to the Gentiles; it was time to take the truth to them, and a miracle was necessary to convince Peter to preach it to them. Peter learned the lesson. He said in Acts 10:34-35: "In truth I perceive that God shows no partiality. But in every nation whoever fears Him and works righteousness is accepted by Him." God shows no partiality ("is no respecter of persons," KJV) and, as His disciples, we must not either. Prejudice, for any reason, is wrong - social, financial, racial, cultural.

No such division should exist in the Lord's kingdom. There is no excuse for those places that have black churches and white churches. The Lord has only one church, and we are all part of it. Do you think there will be red, yellow, black, and white sections in heaven? "... where there is neither Greek nor Jew, circumcised nor uncircumcised, barbarian, Scythian, slave nor free, but Christ is all and in all" (Colossians 3:11).

Do you remember the lesson Paul delivered in the first-century city of Athens, Greece, about God and His nature? In describing God's role as Creator of the universe, he made this statement: "And He has made from one blood every nation of men to dwell on all the face of the earth, and has determined their preappointed times and the boundaries of their dwellings" (Acts 17:26). All human beings, no matter what their color or racial makeup, descended from "one blood." If a person needs a blood transfusion for medical purposes, it can be from anyone. They do not segregate donor blood as black, white, brown, Asian, Indian, Native American, Jewish, Chinese, Korean, Vietnamese, etc. White supremacists can receive blood transfusions or organ transplants from anyone, even if they don't like it.

Many believe that there really is no such thing as race at all. Many of the physical differences we see in the world around us can be attributed to millennia of changes under different climate and cultural circumstances that resulted from genetic pooling. When God scattered the languages of the people in Genesis 11, after the incident at the Tower of Babel, people and cultures likely chose to live around those who spoke the

Radically Integrated Churches

same language. As the decades and centuries passed, those pooled groups of people likely began to intermarry and produce new genetic combinations, distinct from those in other pooled groups in different parts of the world. Genesis 9 tells us about the world in the post-flood era and explains how the three sons of Noah, located in various parts of the world, began to develop characteristics (we would call them racial qualities) through intermarrying with those who also lived around them. However, they all descended from Shem, Ham, and Japheth (that's the central message of Genesis 10), who descended from Noah and his wife, who ultimately themselves, were descendants of Adam and Eve. Don't forget that the name Eve means "the mother of all living" (Genesis 3:20).

One of the lessons we learn in the New Testament is that Jesus came to save all people. It doesn't matter to Him what someone's skin color is or what language they speak or any of the other small differences that may separate or distinguish us from one another. The church of Jesus Christ is a universal body that welcomes anyone. The Great Commission states, "Go into all the world and preach the gospel to every creature" (Mark 16:15). Every human being has an immortal soul that is separated from God by sin and requires forgiveness. When a person obeys the gospel of Christ, they are added to the universal church by God (Acts 2:47). Every Christian on the face of the whole earth is made in God's image and is a part of the one body for which Jesus died on the cross.

We often sing the song that says, "The Blessed Gospel is for all." We need to really mean it when we sing that song together in praise of the LORD Almighty.

If we want to convince society to be color-blind, the church can show the world that we can worship together, get along with each other, and love one another in the Lord's church. We can show them that we are truly disciples of the Messiah by the love that we demonstrate, not just in words but also in our actions (John 13:34-35; 1 John 3:16-18), no matter what race someone is.

"For you are all sons of God through faith in Christ Jesus. For as many of you as were baptized into Christ have put on Christ. There is neither Jew nor Greek, there is neither slave nor free, there is neither male nor female; for you are all one in Christ Jesus" (Galatians 3:26-28).

NOTES

DAY 24

Effective Teacher Training

Think back to your days in elementary and high school. You probably remember some teachers who really touched your life in a profound way. Others, not so much. The same principle holds true when it comes to teaching Bible classes. Some teachers make a life-changing difference in their students' lives; others fill the time period but don't really have much impact. Which kind of teacher do you think God wants us to be? And how can we help more sincere disciples to be the kind of powerful Bible teachers that so many people, both adults and children, need?

Nothing can replace a deep understanding of the Bible. Teachers must know how the whole Bible fits together and contains a single story from Genesis to Revelation. It is one book composed of sixty-six smaller books that tell a unified story, ultimately bringing us to faith in Jesus the Messiah (Galatians 3:24). The whole Bible is about Jesus.

Some of our Bible knowledge can come from the regular Bible classes we attend and sermons we hear. If the church has a good teaching program in place for all ages, then you should eventually (within a relatively short time, less than ten years) study your way through the entire Bible. If you study hard and take good notes, you should have your own set of study tools all the way through the scriptures. If you are also teaching off and on during that time, you might have to get a set of recorded lessons (maybe on CD, YouTube, or the church's website) to catch up on the classes you have missed. Many churches try to repeat good classes rather than just having them be a one-time shot, so maybe you won't have to miss any studies at all. That takes good leadership in charge of the teaching for the church; hopefully, where you worship there is someone in charge of the teaching program who really loves the job and is good at arranging the classes to guide everyone through the Bible in a reasonable amount of time.

If the church's regular teaching program doesn't cover something you are going to teach, then find a workbook or study guide that is commercially available and study your way through it in advance so that when your turn comes to teach, you will have a good head start on the material. A lot of very good, well-written study materials are out there that you can buy. Be proactive and work ahead, even if the people in charge aren't as helpful as you wish they were.

Many churches have developed a resource room that contains materials studied in the past, supplies, maybe even videos and other helpful study tools that one can use. If the church follows a three or four year rotation in the children's classes, then the same material can be used, over and over again by teachers working with a completely different class from the students who went over the material four years ago. If something was really good for one class, it should be great for the next one that will go through the lessons. You shouldn't have to start from scratch to teach a class, unless a new program is being implemented. Even then, many of the lessons will probably be the same Bible stories in a new series as they were in an older one. There are only so many ways to study and organize a class about the judges, the kings, or the prophets.

Nothing beats adequate preparation. Some people have enough Bible knowledge to "wing it" through the class period. But how much better would it be for everyone if all our teachers put a lot of time, preparation, prayer, and thought into every class?

If you are not currently teaching a Bible class, but you would really like to get involved, just jump in and get involved. Ask a good teacher if you could work with him or her in a quarter (or trimester) of class. Be present for every class, participate, work, and study as though you were the one in charge. Listen and watch the things that the experienced teacher does that seem to work really well, or even observe if some things don't seem to click with the class. Maybe you and the other teacher could get together in person, on-line, or over the phone and discuss ideas about how the next class period should go. Don't be afraid to learn from others who do a great job of helping the students learn from the word of God. You don't have to say a word in the class itself; just prepare and then sit back and listen. Volunteer outside of class to cut up visual aids, copy a page, or call someone who is struggling to attend and let them know you are looking forward to seeing them in class. Anything that will help the teacher be ready for the session is appreciated. Maybe the next quarter, in the same class, you could volunteer to help another teacher, and then you can compare (in your own mind) the job that both teachers did and take the best of both of them to form your own style of teaching.

Effective Teacher Training

There can also be value in conducting teacher training classes. Two possible ways to hold such classes would be to teach the Bible itself (maybe the church has never had a class on the Minor Prophets, the book of Revelation, or Psalms) or to have a class on teaching techniques. I have taught both types of training classes, and each has its own distinct benefits. For younger children's classes, below middle school age (twelve and under), it would be more beneficial to have a qualified woman teacher to direct the training classes. Most of us men are not as experienced at teaching younger students as women are, and they may have ideas that might never occur to us men. That doesn't mean that more men couldn't teach younger children's classes, but women (many of whom are mothers) are often more patient and kind with little ones, and most children would feel more comfortable with a woman than a man.

Women who teach our children do an invaluable service to the Lord's people. Teaching younger children is a serious job, and we need to understand that what we are talking about is preparing souls for eternity. Little children will soon reach the age of accountability (faster than we often realize). Study habits form early, as do adult personality traits and the attitudes our children will have toward God and His Word. Teaching the Bible is the single, most important work in the world, and frankly, more so for children than for adults.

A couple of quick tips for teachers for both adults and children.

Take some time to consider how you will begin the class. A thought-provoking introduction will capture the students' interest and make the class something they want to learn. Strive for excellence here and come up with an approach that will grab their attention and hopefully keep it high for the entire class period.

You also need a challenging conclusion, with a personal goal for everyone to accomplish, based on the Bible study itself. This challenge will include a list of things to do or something to work on in response to the lesson that has been taught. (And, of course, the stuff in between the introduction and conclusion is important also.)

Emphasize one take-home lesson in each study. If you try to have the students remember ten points from each class, they probably won't recall any of them the next day. But if you emphasize one thing from each session, it will hopefully stick with them until the next study, or perhaps even longer. If you teach only one class per week, you have driven home fifty lessons per year. That would be a pretty good achievement.

Strengthening the Local Church

Nothing contributes to the strength of a church like its teaching program. The teaching program is perhaps the single most important part of our work. We cannot afford to lose an entire generation of young people, as so many local churches have done. The Bible class program is the best way to prepare the leaders of the future.

NOTES

DAY 25

Leadership: Relationships and Influence

One of the church's greatest needs today is leadership. No organization, including the Lord's church, can rise above its leadership. There are many different thoughts about leadership, and I want to discuss this idea from a biblical perspective. (Any time there is a difference between what the world tells us and what God says on the subject, we should always go with God.) Many really good churches with great potential have been brought down by poor leadership. When you read Luke 22:24-27, you see immediately that there is a huge difference in how the world views leadership and how the Lord does. So what is leadership?

To the world, it is a title, like benefactor, boss, CEO, supervisor, etc. Some people just want an important title. To them, it is a position, the opportunity to be "over" other people. The more people work under you, the more important you are. In the business world, leadership may include being "cut-throat," doing anything to get to the top. You can mistreat others if necessary; lie about them if it helps make you look better; undercut others, however you need to. It is being "the alpha male," the one everybody thinks is someone special. It's all about you and making yourself look and feel important and powerful.

To the Lord, leadership is serving others, helping people, and being there when someone else needs you. It is the influence you have to encourage others to do the right thing. That's why relationships are crucial to real leadership. In true leadership, it's about helping others become all they can be. It is not about power at all, unless it is in the sense of helping others develop their own power to succeed spiritually.

The main point you need to understand is this: Everyone can be a leader of others. This is not simply something for elders, preachers, deacons, or some kind of "church officials." Every Christian can take charge of a given situation and help lead others to make the right decisions. We do that by forming relationships with people and then using our godly influence to encourage them to choose God's way, rather than the way of the world. Think about it. Who are you most influenced by, your friends or people you don't even know? Let's look at some verses from the New Testament about our influence in the lives of others.

Strengthening the Local Church

Matthew 5:13-16 describes our influence in two ways, as the salt of the earth and the light of the world. Both are interesting word pictures. The purpose is to glorify God (not us), according to verse 16. The greater the darkness, the more the light of the world is needed and the brighter it shines (imagine a match in a brightly lit room compared to one in a dark room).

Read Philippians 1:20. We often sing a song that says, "Let the Beauty of Jesus Be Seen in Me." He reminds us that in nothing should we be ashamed of our relationship with the Lord. With all boldness, stand up for the truth and what is right. And again, the goal is that Christ will be magnified in all things.

People may argue against what you try to teach them, but they cannot argue against a godly example of a person who is seeking to glorify the Lord by his actions. Albert Schweitzer said, "Example is not the main thing in influencing others. It is the only thing."

In 1 Timothy 4:12, Paul shows that young people have this responsibility as well as older people. Paul specifies areas of life where young people can set a good example for others—"in word, in conduct, in love, in spirit, in faith, in purity."

In Titus 2:9-10, the apostle talks to slaves about their relationship with their masters. He says their lives should "adorn the doctrine." The NIV translates that phrase as "so that in every way they will make the teaching about God our Savior attractive." That's how we should live, so others find our lives attractive. Never forget that others will follow your example before they will follow your advice.

Revelation 14:13 teaches that your influence will live on even after your death ("their works follow them"). What do you remember about George Washington, Abraham Lincoln, or Adolf Hitler? What do you remember about the apostle Paul, Barnabas, or Timothy? What do you remember about Jezebel, Lot's wife, or Judas Iscariot? What will people remember about you?

My mother passed away suddenly and unexpectedly on October 8, 2021. I had talked to her the night before on the phone, and we had talked about the Bible and how important it is to live by its teachings. I spoke a few days later at her funeral service and used her little Bible that she read every day. The ribbon marker had been placed at the scripture that reminds us to set a good example for others, which my mother always tried to do. "A good name is to be chosen rather than great riches" (Proverbs 22:1).

The point of all of this is to give the world a godly example to follow (not a perfect example), but one of a person who is trying to do right (1 Corinthians 11:1). That is spiritual leadership, and you don't have to be an elder to have that kind of godly influence on others. Consider some applications of those we should try to influence.

1) Neighbors, co-workers
Do they even know you are a Christian? How can they tell? Do you act like one around them? Do you uplift them by your good example? Have you ever invited them to study or to attend services? You don't have to be doing this all the time, but have you ever?

2) Friends and classmates
Again, can they tell you are different from others because you are a Christian? Do you use bad language, gossip about others, lie to your teachers, or do ungodly things like drink alcohol or even use drugs?

3) Our children (Ephesians 6:4)
Satan won't hesitate to influence them in the wrong direction. Are you trying to help them learn to love and obey God?

4) Other family members
Maybe your parents (I have seen weak parents be changed by the influence of their children), in-laws, grandparents, aunts, uncles, and cousins. You can help others be stronger and better by your godly example.

5) Other Christians
What does your example of faithfulness tell others about how much they should love the Lord? Do you pass notes at services or take notes in class or from the sermon? Do you whisper and laugh through the lesson and songs? Do you sleep in class? What is your example teaching others?

Again, I want you to see that this is an area where you can be a spiritual leader to others. Through the relationships that you already have, you can set a positive, godly example for others and influence their eternal fate. Example alone will not convert people to Christ; they still need to be taught the gospel. But a good example does draw people to Him who will be more receptive to the truth because they have seen it lived out in your life. You will influence others with your example. It is up to you if it will be for good or for bad, a positive or a negative influence.

NOTES

DAY 26

Appointing Elders and Deacons

Most men are going to be intimidated by the idea of serving as an elder. It is a very serious responsibility, not something to be taken lightly, but only to glorify God and help people make it to heaven. If a person wants to be an elder for selfish purposes, to be in charge, and to be able to boss other people around, he is completely missing the whole point.

It is always easier, with less pressure on all the families involved, if the church is looking to appoint additional men as elders or deacons, rather than establishing the positions in the church. If you have a couple or three elders, thinking about appointing one or two more is not worrisome. Hopefully, you can. But, if you can't, the church still has elders. However, if you do not have an eldership and want to try to appoint two or three, that can be more difficult. Same thing with choosing men to be deacons, but maybe a little less pressure all the way around there than trying to appoint shepherds for the flock. It is especially hard to do some of this if the church has never had official leaders and servants, or if it had some thirty years ago, but hasn't had anyone serve God in that capacity for a long time.

A preaching friend of mine is fond of saying that the best time to plant an apple tree is twenty-five years ago. The second-best time is today. So, if the church didn't start working toward having scripturally qualified men to lead the church twenty-five years ago, the next best time to work on that is right now. If the church thinks they might have men qualified to serve in five years, they should not wait four and a half years to start working toward that goal. They should start now.

It might be helpful for the preacher, if you have one, to meet with any men who are qualified, close to being qualified, or who think they are qualified and have some Bible studies together. Be upfront about the purpose of the time together and allow them to attend or decline to attend, based on their inclination toward serving the Lord in this way.

Study the qualifications together. The scriptural requirements for serving are found in 1 Timothy 3:1-7 and Titus 1:5-9 for elders, and in 1 Timothy 3:8-13 for deacons. Lots of word studies, definitions, and discussions about the qualifications and their meanings should be done. Don't hold anything back, including reservations from the men themselves or from the other people in the group. Use your own judgment about whether to include their wives at first, or wait until the actual time for appointment might be nearer.

Do not rush through this step. If there is any uncertainty about even one of the qualifications, make certain the whole group comes to an agreement about it. You don't want to get right down to being ready to appoint two men to be elders, only to find out that one of them has concerns about the other one.

If the preacher and any men who want to participate get past this first stage, the next thing I would personally recommend is studying Max Dawson's workbook, *Kingdom Leaders*. This study might be done with just this group or it might be helpful to have the congregation study this material together so that everyone has the opportunity to think about, study about, and pray about the options that lie before the church. It will be important, not only for the men who will be working together to lead the church, but for those who will be serving God under their oversight, that all be on the same page. Again, there should be no surprises late in the process. Solve any and all problems that might exist long before you get ready to act. (My personal favorite part of Max's study is when he discusses Ezekiel 34 and how the leaders of Israel in the Old Testament were shepherds who took care of themselves, but not the sheep. That part alone is worth the price of the book. The whole book is really good.)

I have taught some material on leadership based on the book of Nehemiah. This man of God took a very difficult situation, turned it around, and succeeded in accomplishing what God wanted them to do. There are several good studies based on Nehemiah, and any of them can form the basis for a profitable study on leading other people. He wasn't perfect, and everyone didn't respond appropriately to the will of God in every situation, but he was a good leader who did much for God and His people.

On Day 18 of this study, I wrote some things about important leadership principles. You might find it helpful to go back and re-read that information in connection with this discussion.

Yesterday, we talked about a general kind of leadership, that is, the influence that we all have in the lives of the people we know. It is important for every Christian to set the right kind of example for people outside of Christ, so that our godliness might help draw them to learn more about Him. Today, of course, we are talking about the God-given official role of elders (and deacons).

It is a blessing to work in a growing church under scripturally qualified, serving elders who truly watch out for the souls of the members. Sometimes churches will appoint men to serve as elders, and then, rather than supporting and encouraging them, they will fuss, fight, argue, and criticize them for every decision they make. Be thankful for them, make allowances for their imperfections, and be supportive in every possible way. Cooperate with them and certainly remember to pray for them and their families. It isn't easy to be a shepherd, and stubborn, uncooperative sheep make it even harder.

Many of the passages that tell us about the duties and responsibilities of church elders also remind us of our obligation as members of the local church who will work under their oversight. No one can be a good leader if others do not follow well.

It might be helpful, both for the men who are considering becoming elders and for everyone else, for that matter, to do some character studies of some of the leaders who are talked about in the Bible, both testaments. Of course, they did not serve in the same capacity as elders today, but they did lead others, sometimes quite well and sometimes not so well. Make a list of their successes and failures, their virtues and faults. Look at the lives of people like Moses, Joshua, Caleb, the Judges, the Kings, the prophets. Max Dawson's workbook, *Kingdom Leaders*, mentioned earlier, has a number of lessons that are helpful "case studies" of both good and bad leadership. There are valuable applications from both directions that can help today's leaders learn from others. It is said that the average man learns from his own mistakes, the wise man learns from the mistakes of others, and some men just never learn. Which one of those would you like to be?

Let me take a moment and point out to you that many elders in the early church were paid financially by the church for their work. 1 Timothy 5:17-20 quotes the Savior Himself, who said that a worker is worthy of his wages (verse 18). An elder is not supposed to be "greedy for money" (1 Timothy 3:3). Of course, no Christian is supposed to be greedy for money, but it seems to me that Paul includes that in the qualifications because a person could have been tempted by the financial support he might get if he is appointed as an elder. Not every church can afford to pay their elders, but a fulltime elder can do much good for the kingdom if they don't have the distraction of a 40-50-hour-per-week job.

NOTES

DAY 27

Merging for Greater Effectiveness

It is just my opinion, but I am convinced that one medium-sized congregation can accomplish more for God than two smaller churches.

It only makes sense that if you have more people, you have more teachers, song leaders, personal workers, more possibilities for elders and deacons, more people to practice hospitality, and on and on the list goes.

Let me start by saying there are some advantages to smaller churches. There can be more opportunities for men to serve publicly; this often helps to develop untapped talent that may be overlooked in larger groups. Having two churches in a large city may mean that you have more opportunities to reach outsiders who may not be willing to drive longer distances to attend a church that is farther away. It is harder for a shy person to get lost in the crowd when the crowd is not very large to begin with.

However, I believe there are many more advantages to larger churches. You can have a better teaching program because you have more qualified teachers to choose from. You can have larger classes, which can create more helpful discussions and more friendships among students, both young and old. You can have more young people in a large group which, again, gives them more chances for friends within the church and maybe even more choices when it comes to choosing a spouse as they get older. You have more qualified men to choose from for elders and deacons (starting another church sometimes dissolves elderships). The contribution is typically higher in larger churches, which enables them to support more preachers in weak areas of the world. If two churches merge, they should only need one preacher, and the other one can move to another church to help alleviate and reduce the preacher shortage. If you only have one building and expenses to support, that should save some of the Lord's money as well.

There are often two churches in relatively close proximity because the two groups didn't get along in the past. Sometimes this is because of doctrinal differences, and those issues would still need to be studied and worked out. That is easier said than done, of course. Some people may need to swallow their pride, and some old wounds might have to be healed; again, that can be a real challenge at times. But we follow the same Bible, we believe the same basic things, we serve the same God, and we have been redeemed by the same Savior. Surely, those big things are more important than the little differences that often keep us apart. I don't mean to trivialize anything; I realize how easily close relationships can be fractured, and it is really hard to forgive others when we are convinced that they are the offending party.

I have spoken with groups like this over the years. They separated years ago (the reason doesn't really matter), and the people involved say that it will never be any better until there are "a few more funerals." Some people really hold a grudge for a long time, and it is never easy to change our minds about something (that's even more true as we grow older, isn't it?). That is really sad to think about.

But we are talking about the Lord's church here. It is not our church, based on our ideas and our personal preferences. It's all about Him and the plan that He has laid out for us in the New Testament.

There have been times in the past when two groups within a single church couldn't work through their differences, and as a result, one group decided to start a new congregation on the other side of town. It is true that some people are just really hard to get along with, and someone who has that kind of heart and attitude is not very Christ-like. But to promote division and try to make it look like the church is prospering so well that we just have to start a new group in a new area is hypocrisy. Several of the "works of the flesh" (Galatians 5:19-21) deal with the problems of jealousy, divisiveness, and enmity toward our brothers and sisters in the Lord. Paul tells us that "those who practice such things will not inherit the kingdom of God." Division is not something to play around with; it is serious business. Paul says that souls will be lost for this type of disposition and actions.

I am very much in favor of starting new congregations where they are needed. A new work can often show growth, strength, and unity. However, starting a new church just so you don't have to put up with people who have irritated you is not godly. Such actions and behavior do not glorify the Lord.

Sometimes we grow by trying to reach an area where there is no faithful church. But other times, when our motives are not pure and our desires are not in keeping with God's will, it is sinful to separate from people with whom we should be united. Plant a new church in a new area where the gospel has not yet reached. But maybe what is needed in some areas is for two small, struggling congregations to unite under one roof, and everybody will be stronger and better off.

Real estate and buildings are expensive. It used to be that a church could purchase a piece of property, build a church building with an auditorium, classrooms, and parking space, with room to grow for a reasonable price that wouldn't take too long to pay off. Maybe in some other parts of the world, that is still the situation, but in the United States, it is very expensive to do that now. We have never had a lot of really wealthy members, so, in a lot of places that's why many of our church buildings are found in out-the-way, off-the-beaten-path, locations. High visibility property on Main Street is hard to come by and expensive to maintain. We just try to do the best we can with what we have.

The desire for merging should come out of a desire to see God glorified in His church. "Now to Him who is able to do exceedingly abundantly above all that we ask or think, according to the power that works in us, to Him be glory in the church by Christ Jesus to all generations, forever and ever" (Ephesians 3:20-21).

If the best we have to offer God is eight members who meet in a home, and some of the members have to drive an hour or more to get there, then may God richly bless you in all you do for Him. I am not, in any way, trying to make smaller churches feel badly about doing the best they can for God. He loves you, and I am grateful for all you do.

But if less than ten miles away, another house has eight members who are struggling and discouraged, then just maybe it could work out for those two groups to merge and serve the heavenly Father. Wouldn't that be an encouragement for everyone?

Wherever we worship, let's not forget to do what we can to bring other people into a saving knowledge of Jesus the Messiah. Remember to invite people to "come and see" (John 1:46). Growing is always the best remedy for a small church.

Much good can come out of a merger, if it is done with the proper spirit. It will lift hearts and help us to overcome an attitude of discouragement and defeatism. It will help us to do more together and increase our work for God.

NOTES

DAY 28

Leading Public Prayer

There are three basic types of prayers that are regularly led in our worship services: opening prayer, closing prayer, and Lord's Supper prayers. There are also special prayers that are often part of our assemblies: at a baptism, accompanying a restoration and for a serious illness situation. For those who lead these prayers, please consider these thoughts about leading those prayers.

1. Remember that you are leading everyone else in prayer. This is not a personal prayer where you should ask for Bill's, sisters', aunt's, daughter in law's best friend. This is why it is usually best to use phrases like "we pray" and not "I pray." You want to say things that will help everyone feel like they can say, Amen, as their own prayer, not like they have overheard a personal conversation between you and God. (We ought to pray those kinds of prayers on our own, of course, but not while we are leading a public prayer for the whole church.)

2. Speak loudly enough to be heard. Do not forget that, with your head bowed, if you speak in hushed tones, the sound will go straight down to your feet and not be projected out into the auditorium or classroom where everyone can hear it. Many people are a little bit shy and don't like to be upfront of the whole group, but this is why it is usually helpful to go to a microphone to pray, so everyone can hear. (Unless, you are praying in an Amazon Rainforest setting where they don't have a public address system.) Again, everyone needs to hear what is said so they can add their own Amen, either out loud or privately to themselves. So don't yell at the top of your voice, but speak loudly enough so the others can hear what you are praying for.

3. Do not talk too fast. This is one of the main symptoms of stage fright, especially for beginners and it is something that should get easier as time goes on and you get more experienced at praying in front of others. Don't rush through the things you need to say during the prayer and then finish it with a quick "In Jesus' name, Amen" in rapid final flourish. Speak slowly enough so everyone can hear every word. That doesn't mean it should be tedious and boring sounding, only that everyone knows what is being said.

4. Pray like you talk. Some people have learned, through listening to the prayers of others, a lot of old, worn-out, repetitive phrases that include King James era (A.D. 1611) language. Most of us do not greet our family and friends these days by saying, "How are thou"? So why do we talk to God that way? I know that some people feel it is more respectful to say thee and thou and thine to God, but those are not religious terms that apply exclusively to God. It was the common way people spoke to each other, not just in prayer, back when the King James Version and the Old American Standard Version were translated. If you truly believe it is disrespectful not to refer to God as "Thou" and "Thine," there is nothing wrong with it. But there is also nothing wrong with using "You" and "Your" either. It can be hard to make the verbs fit the pronouns when we use the older style and, for the most part, it would be easier to just pray the same way you talk. That's what prayer is, talking with God. As long as we do so in a reverent and respectful way, You and Your are fine.

"What is the conclusion then? I will pray with the spirit and I will also pray with the understanding. I will sing with the spirit, and I will also sing with the understanding. Otherwise, if you bless with the spirit, how will he who occupies the place of the uninformed say 'Amen' at your giving of thanks, since he does not understand what you say? For you indeed give thanks well, but the other is not edified" (1 Corinthians 14:15-17).

5. Do not "show off" when you are leading public prayer. Some men use a completely different voice when they pray; it is almost as though they are trying to impress the hearers of the prayer rather than simply addressing God. "And when you pray, you shall not be like the hypocrites. For they love to pray standing in the synagogues and on the corners of the streets, that they may be seen by men. Assuredly, I say to you, they have their reward" (Matthew 6:6). If you are trying to entertain others when you are supposed to be leading the group in prayer, you have the wrong motive in your heart. Do not pray publicly if your purpose is to be "seen by men."

6. Do not go on and on, if there is no reason for it. Admittedly, sometimes there are quite a few things that need to be prayed for, but most of the time, a shorter, more thought-out prayer, will suffice. "And when you pray, do not use vain repetitions as the heathen do. For they think that they will be heard for their many words" (Matthew 6:7). At times, it might be helpful to mention all the sick people you want God to bless, but at other times, if their names and situations

Leading Public Prayer

were just listed in the preceding announcements, you don't really need to name them all again. A simple, "please bless those who were just mentioned as being sick" will be enough. "Vain repetitions" does not mean that you cannot mention something you have prayed for before, but it could include saying the same thing over and over in the same prayer. Just be careful not to do that.

The "Model Prayer," often called the Lord's prayer only contains 66 words (in some translations). But it includes a lot in a short prayer. Again, Jesus warns against thinking that longer is always better when He says, "they think that they will be heard for their many words." We have probably all been in assemblies where the prayer leader just went on and on and on. That doesn't usually enhance the prayer, rather it detracts from it.

7. Do not forget to pray to the Father through Jesus Christ. "And whatever you do in word or deed, do all in the name of the Lord Jesus, giving thanks to God the Father through Him" (Colossians 3:17). In a prayer for the bread at the Lord's Supper, we should pray that it helps us to remember Jesus' body (not Your body, addressed to the Father) and the fruit of the vine recalls Christ's blood shed (not God the Father's blood or "Your blood"). God the Father did not die on the cross; Jesus the Son did and we pray through Him to the heavenly Father.

In Luke 11:1, the disciples of Jesus asked Him, "Lord, teach us to pray." When we are leading others in public prayer, we should be mindful of the setting and the need to address God for everyone in the assembly. We should speak to God with a sense of devotion and reverence (Hebrews 12:28-29), to the very best of our ability.

We should approach God humbly, not to seen by others and we should think of everyone's needs and feelings when we are addressing God. The model prayer of Jesus (Matthew 6:9-13) is addressed to "Our Father in heaven, Hallowed be Your name." The word, hallowed, means respected, admired, reverend, holy, awesome. This is not something to be taken lightly.

NOTES

DAY 29

Paying the Price for World Evangelism

"Go into all the world and preach the gospel to every creature" (Mark 16:15). Do you remember who told you to do that? It is Jesus; it's in red letters and everything. How are you doing so far? Have you at least talked with your neighbor? It has to start somewhere, and going into all the neighborhood is a better beginning than just ignoring what the Savior tells you to do.

Most of us are not going to move our families to some place halfway around the world. Someone needs to do that. However, they are going to need some financial help to go somewhere and start a new church. So, the two options for most Christians are "go and preach" or "stay and pay." If we cannot go ourselves, we surely have some responsibility to help financially support those who do make the sacrifice and go. He didn't say we have to finance the whole operation all by ourselves, but we do need to do what we can to help.

I know of a church in central Illinois with a local preacher who has been able to do other work to help support himself financially. He has preached at this congregation for several years with a relatively small amount of local pay. A significant part of their weekly contribution goes directly to the support of a faithful preacher, in this case, in Russia. He is a Russian-born citizen who was converted a few years ago and who wants to help his fellow Russians learn the truth. The group in Russia is relatively small and unable to give him much pay from their church, and he needs outside help to do this vital work. This (also small) church in Illinois is doing what they can to promote their part of world evangelism. For a small church, they have a really good contribution because these members have been taught the value and importance of spreading the gospel around the entire globe. It is important to them.

There are several things that American Christians can do to help the cause around the world.

We all need to pray for preachers and their families who go to other countries to share the faith. Those of us who have never done this likely have no idea how difficult it is for parents and children to move to a place where they probably do not know the language, where they will have to learn local customs that are very different from America, probably will have to homeschool the children and will not be able to spend every holiday with parents, grandparents, uncles and aunts, cousins, and the friends the children have known early in life. It is just a gigantic sacrifice on the part of those faithful Christians who decide to do that. They really need our prayers, and they need to know that we have prayed for them and will continue to do so specifically.

We also really need to write to them. They may very well have access to modern technology, so we might be able to text them or send them emails of encouragement, but not every place where the gospel needs to go has those conveniences yet. A personal letter may take a long time to get to them, and some may never get to the proper destination. Still, we should try to communicate with them however we can that we are thinking about them and appreciate what they are doing for the Lord and admire their courage and determination to take the gospel to unreached people. Do not gripe to them about your first-world problems, because we don't want to do anything that would discourage them, make their work harder, or leave them feeling even more lonely than they already are. But do assure them of your love, appreciation, and your prayers on their behalf. And then, don't just say you are, but really pray for them.

It would also be nice for children to write to their children. Maybe your children are young enough and about the same age as their children, and you could have them write occasional notes to their friends. You can decide whether it would be best for them to do that monthly, weekly, or every other week. However, it would be good for the children, and their parents would be so grateful knowing that other children are thinking about their kids and want to pick up their spirits. If the church supports preaching families in other parts of the world, some of the children's Bible classes could draw cards, write letters, and maybe even send little gifts to the kids of the family from time to time. It wouldn't take much time out of the class to do something like that. Good teachers at that level would probably have some really great ideas, better than my own, to help these sacrificial families.

Denominational groups (missionary societies and missions boards, etc.) send lots of money overseas to spread their false doctrines around the world. We believe, rightly so in my opinion, that those human organizations are without Bible authority, and we preach sermons showing why we think it is the duty of the church of Jesus Christ to teach the saving gospel to a lost world. But our job is more than just preaching against an unscriptural arrangement for doing something. We have to obey the right way to do these things and make certain that we are taking the gospel to lost souls everywhere. We need to stand against false teaching (1 John 4:1 and lots of other verses). But we will not be able to stand before the judgment seat of Christ and proudly proclaim, "Lord, we didn't use unscriptural methods; we didn't fall for human organized missionary societies; we didn't use sponsoring church arrangements against Your will; we didn't get involved with entertainment and false methods of drawing large crowds; we didn't do any of those things that the man-made human denominations did." (And please, realize that I don't think we should do any of those unscriptural methods either.) But, the question will be, alright then, what did you do? Did you do your part in going into the world and sharing the gospel with the lost?

I realize that small churches may feel like they don't have enough money to do much in this area. But, with the exception of very, very small groups, most churches would likely have an extra $100 a month to send to a needy and worthy preacher somewhere. That's not a lot of money to us, but it might be the difference between survival and death to a family in a remote part of Africa, Asia, Latin America, or even Europe. If we had any idea how little some people in other parts of the world have, we would be ashamed that we didn't do more with what we have to help others.

Preachers from America who travel around the world to preach often come back with some of the saddest stories you couldn't even imagine in your wildest dreams about the living conditions of some of our brothers and sisters and their families in other places. I usually end up crying like a baby when they show pictures of starving children, sacrificing parents, or struggling Christians who are doing their best just to survive with almost nothing: little or no food, no home, barely enough clothing to cover themselves decently. Many times, they don't have clean water to drink and certainly no access to medical care for the sick and dying. Starvation, dehydration, persecution from unbelievers, they face extreme heat or cold with so little in the way of human comforts. We take so much for granted and often feel little appreciation for all the material blessings we have been given by God.

We need to send more preachers to more places in an attempt to save more souls. We need to send more money to native preachers, those who are been converted to Christ and who want to do all they can to help save their fellow citizens around the world. We often don't realize

Strengthening the Local Church

how much of a difference a little support can make for them. They already know the language, they already live among the lost people, and it doesn't look like we are trying to import a new American or Western religion to their land. Bigger churches can do more, but even smaller churches can do something. We have the ability today to help turn the world upside down. Yet, we are often complacent, lukewarm, and uncaring about lost souls who are dying and will face a Christ-less eternity. We have to do better.

NOTES

DAY 30

Generous Giving

Giving is often an unpopular subject. Preachers usually avoid saying much about giving because they don't want to be accused of "preaching for the money." Many preachers could make a lot more money doing something else, but their hearts are fixed on serving God and saving souls. It is almost always a financial sacrifice for a man who devotes his life to full-time gospel work.

And many preachers are very much underpaid in return for giving their whole life to God. They don't do it to get rich quickly, but they deserve to be taken care of in return for doing the most important work in the world. I heard a preacher once say that his father, also a preacher, was told that the goal of every church should be to get the best preaching possible for the least amount of money. How generous some people are! If a worker is worthy of his wages (and Jesus said he is, in Luke 10:7), we should not make preachers try to scrape by on poverty-level salaries. Things have been getting better in recent years, but maybe we need to do even better still.

Most things now cost more than they used to. There is general inflation in society over time, and so, most churches will be spending more money than before, even if they aren't doing much new. Also, I have suggested a number of (I hope) valuable changes that some groups might want to make, and very few of them will be cost neutral.

So, like it or not, if we are going to discuss church revival and renewal, we must talk about the church's contribution. As a brief reminder, here are a few of the verses that speak to the subject of our giving.

"Now concerning the collection for the saints, as I have given orders to the churches of Galatia, so you must do also. On the first day of the week let each one of you lay something aside, storing up as he may prosper, that there be no collections when I come" (1 Corinthians 16:1-2).

"But this I say: He who sows sparingly will also reap sparingly, and he who sows bountifully will also reap bountifully. So let each one give as he purposes in his heart, not grudgingly or of necessity; for God loves a cheerful giver" (2 Corinthians 9:6-7).

"Moreover, brethren, we make known to you the grace of God bestowed on the churches of Macedonia: that in a great trial of affliction the abundance of their joy and their deep poverty abounded in the riches of their liberality. For I bear witness that according to their ability, yes, and beyond their ability, they were freely willing, imploring us with much urgency that we would receive the gift and the fellowship of the ministering to the saints. And not only as we had hoped, but they first gave themselves to the Lord, and then to us by the will of God" (2 Corinthians 8:1-5).

One of the duties of the church is to financially support those who preach and teach the gospel. As Jesus emphasizes in Luke 10:7, "a laborer is worthy of his wages." It is this same principle that authorizes the church to pay a secretary, a personal worker, those who clean the building, those who mow the lawn, or paint the building. It is not only authorizing those who do the pulpit preaching for a local church, but for those who do other work for the Lord as well. It is scriptural to pay those who labor to do the work for God that needs to be done in a local church.

"Or is it only Barnabas and I who have no right to refrain from working? Who ever goes to war at his own expense? Who plants a vineyard and does not eat of its fruit? Or who tends a flock and does not drink of the milk of the flock? Do I say these things as a mere man? Or does not the law say the same also? For it is written in the law of Moses, 'You shall not muzzle an ox while it treads out the grain.' Is it oxen God is concerned about? Or does He say it altogether for our sakes? For our sakes, no doubt, this is written, that he who plows should plow in hope, and he who threshes in hope should be partaker of his hope. If we have sown spiritual things for you, is it a great thing if we reap your material things? If others are partakers of this right over you, are we not even more? Nevertheless we have not used this right, but endure all things lest we hinder the gospel of Christ. Do you not know that those who minister the holy things eat of the things of the temple, and those who serve at the altar partake of the offerings of the altar? Even so the Lord has commanded that those who preach the gospel should live from the gospel" (1 Corinthians 9:6-14).

Let's notice some applications of these scriptures.

First, giving is a responsibility of Christians. It is our duty to support the Lord's work through the local church to which we belong.

Second, this giving should be done on the first day of the week. This phrase is restrictive in that it excludes other days. Churches are not set up to be money-raising machines that will accept funds from anybody at any time for any reason. The Bible pattern is that disciples of Jesus give financially to support His work through His church on His day, the first day of the week.

We might make a quick note about tithing. Many churches refer to their contribution as "the tithe." It is true that, in the Old Testament, Israel was required to tithe (give one-tenth of their income) to support the priests and Levites who functioned in the tabernacle and temple. But there is no such teaching in the New Testament. Rather, all Christians are to give as God has prospered them and according to the amount they have purposed in their hearts.

We should have a good attitude giving to God. He has given us all so much, and we should be freely willing, not under compulsion, to give a portion back to Him for His glory. The passage above, from 2 Corinthians 8, talked about the Macedonian Christians and their joy and sincerity in giving to help others. Paul speaks of the abundance of their joy and that they gave beyond their ability. They had first given themselves and their hearts to the Lord, and so, they were "cheerful" givers.

Several passages mention the attitude of our hearts in all of our service to God. Read Matthew 22:35-38; Luke 14:33; Matthew 6:33. Does the Lord come first in your giving? Or does He simply get the leftovers after you have done everything else you wanted to do?

Notice also that these verses about giving emphasize the Bible principle of sacrifice. Are there things you would like to have, but do not, because you give to God (without grudging and bitterness)? "But do not forget to do good and to share, for with such sacrifices God is well pleased" (Hebrews 13:16). Helping other people often takes some sacrifice, doesn't it?

In Acts 2:44-45 and 4:32-37, Luke tells us about some first-century Jesus followers who sold some of their possessions to be able to help finance the Lord's work. Some even sold land and houses (big things) to help. That is sacrifice, brothers and sisters. The Lord commends them for their willingness to give to others. That is what we are talking about, giving because we can help the work of the Lord's church.

NOTES

DAY 31

Standing in the Gap

The prophet Ezekiel lived in difficult times. (Being a prophet always had its challenges for those men and women who served God in that way. It was never an easy job.) He did his work for the Lord during the reign of Nebuchadnezzar in Babylon. Nebuchadnezzar made things rough for everyone. He was cruel, demanding, and ruthless, showing no pity for anyone who got in his way.

Ezekiel was taken into captivity in Babylon during the second wave of captivity, which occurred in 597 B.C. He was one of three prophets God used during this Chaldean era. Jeremiah spoke primarily to the people of God in Judah. Daniel spoke to the leaders of Babylon in Babylon. And Ezekiel's job was to try to encourage the Hebrews who were in Babylon. They had been taken from their homeland into a country where they did not know the language or the customs, and were being used to serve and benefit their captors. If they made a mistake, they could be put to death right on the spot. Ezekiel's job was difficult; he had to try to keep their spirits up in these challenging times.

What they needed was a leader who would remain strong and devoted to God, providing an example of faithfulness for them. "So I sought for a man among them who would make a wall, and stand in the gap before Me on behalf of the land, that I should not destroy it; but I found no one" (Ezekiel 22:30). A man who would stand in the gap. That's what every church needs. Actually, each church needs several people like that, men and women who will not compromise, but who will stand up for God in any and every circumstance, no matter how dispiriting. As the passage indicates, sometimes that person (or persons) is just not available. But God continues to look for those who can bring sanity to a crazy world.

Sometimes things happen in local churches that are discouraging. People disagree. Some people say and do some rather foolish things. Nobody gets their way all the time. There are those who think they are always right and their way is always best, and no one else better get in the way of what they want. Does that remind anyone else of Diotrephes (3 John 9-11)?

Strengthening the Local Church

One of the biggest problems that churches often face is the tendency for people to rely on human wisdom, rather than God's plan. Sometimes, things make sense to us, and it doesn't matter that our ideas are different than God's; we want things to go our way. James spoke to this dichotomy in James 3:16-18. "For where envy and self-seeking exist, confusion and every evil thing are there. But the wisdom that is from above is first pure, then peaceable, gentle, willing to yield, full of mercy and good fruits, without partiality and without hypocrisy. Now the fruit of righteousness is sown in peace by those who make peace."

God's way is not always easy, but it is always right. When Christians are envious of others, when they are seeking their own desires even above God's will and forcing their ideas on others, there is going to be "confusion and every evil thing." The NIV says "disorder and every evil practice."

We need to be reminded that our ideas are always inferior to God's plan. "For My thoughts are not your thoughts, Nor are your ways My ways, says the LORD. For as the heavens are higher than the earth, So are My ways higher than your ways, And My thoughts than your thoughts" (Isaiah 55:8-9).

1 Corinthians 1 has much to say about the value of human wisdom, and most of what it says is not good. God says, through inspiration, "I will destroy the wisdom of the wise, and bring to nothing the understanding of the prudent" (verse 19, a quote from Isaiah 29:14). Most of us are not nearly as smart or clever as we think we are. Verse 20 tells us that God has "made foolish the wisdom of this world." And verse 25 says, "Because the foolishness of God is wiser than men, and the weakness of God is stronger than men." What some people in the first century mistakenly thought was the "foolishness of God" is so far above human wisdom that there really is no comparison. Any time we think we have a better idea than God, we could not possibly be more wrong.

There are local churches that don't have elders because there is no one there who is qualified. Other churches could have shepherds, but they don't because people who aren't qualified to serve in that capacity still want to run things. They realize that if scripturally qualified men are put into office, they (the non-qualified ones) won't be able to control what happens in the church anymore. They want to be in charge, and they know that they will lose their (self-seeking) power if elders are appointed.

Standing in the Gap

What happens, however, is that, without elders who shepherd the church in the manner intended by God, bullies can take over. Those who are the ugliest or yell the loudest or threaten to leave the church with their whole family if they don't get their way are often allowed to dominate and control everything that happens. Never mind that they are not qualified to do the spiritual work that needs to be done in a local church; they want things to be done their way, and they are not afraid to intimidate others to get what they want. Even in cases where elders do serve, they are often unwilling to stand up to these bullies, who can be very forceful and insistent that they will wreak havoc if they aren't obeyed. That's how all bullies work, in homes, in schools, in society, on the job, and in the church. If they cannot stand up to such intimidation from others, these men are not qualified to serve as elders of God's people. No one said being an elder was an easy job with no confrontation.

So, back to this idea of standing in the gap, what does that mean? It seems to indicate that any job that needs to be done, because God says to do it, needs people who are willing to do it. Every church needs people who will see a job that needs to be accomplished and who are willing to jump in and do it. That is standing in the gap.

Being willing to serve might require stretching your comfort zone. There are some things we all do that have become very comfortable for us. We have done them so many times that they are easy. But many jobs, even in the church, are just not like that, especially if we have never done them before. Nothing is easy the first time we try it. Do you remember the first time you tried to ride a bicycle? Do you recall the first time you gave a speech, maybe in a high school or middle school class? Do you remember the first time you ever baked a turkey, grilled a steak, or made homemade cookies? Each successive time you did those things, it got just a little easier. Serving the Lord is much like that. Things that seem challenging at first get easier the more we do them. Teaching, leading singing, preparing communion, and inviting neighbors to study the Bible are just a few of the many tasks that need to be done by those who are willing.

You don't have to be an elder or a deacon or one of their wives to serve God. You just have to be willing to jump in and do what needs to be done. Elders, deacons, preachers, Bible class teachers and others who serve God publicly are always going to be a part of God's plan to save the world. However, many of us who will never serve in those ways can still make a difference in our world and in the lives of others if we are ready to step up and do what we can. You can make an eternal difference in the destiny of lost people you know. There is a whole world out there to take for God. Why not touch a few of the lost souls you know and do what you can to bring them to Jesus?

If you need some suggestions for things you can do for Him, read Romans 12:9-21 and see if there are some things listed there that you could try. Someone once said that it doesn't take much of a person to be a Christian; it just takes all of him there is.

NOTES

DAY 32

The Importance of Unity

"Behold, how good and how pleasant it is for brethren to dwell together in unity!" (Psalm 133:1).

The Lord clearly desires that His people be united. God does not want division or any form of animosity to exist between His children (1 Corinthians 3:1-3). We all know that church problems can be quite discouraging. It seems like Christians ought to get along with each other better than we do sometimes.

Even the churches of the first century had their share of problems. Corinth struggled with problems like preacheritis, sexual immorality, taking others to court, marriage issues, how to observe the Lord's Supper, and those who denied the resurrection. Some of the Thessalonians had quit their jobs to wait for the Second Coming (they were a financial drain on others and promoted idleness that led to many of them becoming busybodies). Some in Galatia were interested in returning to the Old Law. Many other examples show us there has always been a challenge for God's people to remain united and work together in harmony and trust.

Any time you bring two or more people together, there will be differences in opinions, personalities, backgrounds, experiences, and so on. The more people, the more difficulties the group will face.

Please understand that unity does not mean 100% agreement about everything. If we must agree about all things, each Christian is going to have to have their own congregation, with no other members. I do not know any two people who agree on everything, not even a husband and his wife.

In Acts 15:36-40, Paul and Barnabas had a sharp disagreement about whether to take John Mark with them on a second preaching journey. They ended up going in two different directions, with each of them taking others with them. Neither of them decided to start their own sect or party. Neither one decided to become unfaithful to the Lord because the other one didn't agree with him. Neither of them decided to move across town and start a new congregation. There is no indication here that one was right with God and the other was wrong. When they cooled down, they probably even prayed for each other's success.

We read in Galatians 3:26-28 (a passage promoting unity) that Jews and Gentiles in the first century differed in many customs and practices from their past. But they could still be united in one body. Many of the Jews kept some of their customs after their obedience to the gospel. But they did not start a Jewish church and a Gentile church in the same city and then ignore each other from that point on.

In a passage that has caused some division over the years, but was intended to do the exact opposite, Romans 14:1-6 teaches that they did not have to agree on "eating of meats" or "observing days" to be united. They did not divide over these differences. (Even though the non-meat eaters thought the meat eaters were sinning to do so.)

2 Peter 3:18 shows us that there is a maturity factor to consider here. We don't all grow at the same rate. Some have been Christians for a long time (some for decades); others are brand new disciples. We should not expect a new believer to automatically understand everything the same way as a seasoned disciple. Time and study, together with the right attitude, can help here.

Let me suggest some specific examples of things Christians can disagree on and still be in fellowship with each other. (I realize some will not agree with everything I include on this list. Please do not break up our friendship over this). The women's covering, capital punishment, the war question, should Christians observe Christmas in any way, weddings and funerals in a church building, Bible versions, Sunday evening Lord's Supper, and saying a praying before the contribution are all matters of opinion (as I understand them) and should not be the source of division among God's people.

At the same time, unity is not to be had by a compromise of truth. Unity is not a matter of compromising the truth of God's word. Read Galatians 1:6-9 and 2 Peter 3:15-16. We must learn to recognize the difference between the gospel of Christ and our personal opinions.

2 John 9-11 warns us not to go beyond the teachings of Jesus. How to become a Christian, the organization of the church, its work and worship, the deity of Christ, and the inspiration of the Bible are some examples of things that are non-negotiable. We bring the anathema of

God upon ourselves if we change Bible teaching on these things to get along with others.

And unity is not necessarily the same as peace. Unity and peace are not the same thing, although the fact is that those who are united are at peace with one another. But, peace often comes through a compromise of God's truth. We can have peace with everyone in the world if we will compromise our convictions about what the Bible teaches. However, agreeing to disagree on matters of truth is not a sign of Bible unity. We are not free to just ignore what the Bible teaches.

Truth often divides families (Matthew 10:34-36). But in Romans 16:17, we learn that false doctrines can also divide, and we must know and understand God's will for us. It is important to distinguish between matters of faith and matters of opinion.

Unity is when everyone is trying, to the best of their ability, to speak as the oracles of God (1 Peter 4:11). This verse is the basis for the statement that we speak where the Bible speaks and are silent where the Bible is silent. If God doesn't speak, we should not act. If we will do this, without binding personal opinions, we can have unity in the Bible sense. We will continue to study differences and seek to come to common ground based on what the Bible teaches.

In a practical way, we can help promote unity among God's people in two ways.

First, on a personal level, we can try to work out any problems that might exist between us and any other Christian. Passages like Matthew 5:23-24 and Matthew 18:15-17 teach us to get together with those from whom we have become estranged, and as brothers in the Lord, try to work out those differences.

Second, we can, on a congregational level, try to help others within the church who are having trouble getting along. Maybe all two other people need is a mediator who can help them come to a better understanding and relationship with each other. Perhaps you can be that mediator.

As a bonus point, there is also one other helpful thing that we might be able to do. Some of us, but certainly not all of us, might be in a position where we could help two estranged congregations to start to get along with each other again. This is often quite challenging, but not impossible. Maybe you could help with a situation like this.

Strengthening the Local Church

Perhaps this would be a good time for us to begin dreaming bigger dreams and praying bigger prayers. We can advance the cause of Jesus Christ by trying to help everyone get along with others.

NOTES

DAY 33

The Church in the Twenty-First Century

Most of the chapters in this little devotional book have offered ideas to strengthen, build up, and improve the local church. As Christians, our goal in life should be to become what God wants us to be in every aspect of our lives. Collectively, the church can be everything God wants her to be if we follow the pattern He has given us in the New Testament (2 Timothy 1:13). When we read any part of the New Covenant, we should be thinking about how it applies to what we do for the Lord today. We should be able to show book, chapter, and verse for all of our activities in the church.

1. We need to begin with a vision of who we are. That's what this series is intended to help us remember, who we are and who we can be. A faithful congregation is the Lord's Church (that's why we usually call it, the church of Christ). We were promised, purchased, and redeemed by the blood of Jesus Christ, our Savior. We belong to Christ (Acts 20:28). We are the body of Christ (1 Corinthians 12:27). We are the family of God and are supposed to serve as "the pillar and ground of the truth" (1 Timothy 3:15). We are "His own special people" (Titus 2:14). We are special and unique in this sinful world. We are not just another denomination among many. And we must maintain the distinctive nature of the New Testament church as described in the pages of the New Testament. We are a spiritual body with a spiritual job to do.

2. We must have an evangelistic outreach to the lost souls of the world. A church needs to realize what it is supposed to do. We exist to take Christ to the world. 1 Peter 2:9-10 gives a number of descriptions of the church and says we are to "proclaim the praises of Him who called you out of darkness into His marvelous light." That means we must preach the gospel (the good news of salvation) to the lost.

We have the responsibility to sound out the word of God (1 Thessalonians 1:8). This can be done from the pulpit, in the classroom, on the radio, in the newspaper, on television, on the internet, in homes, on the street corner, in public or in private (Acts 5:42). We do pretty well with the public part of that when we listen to a gospel sermon at our Sunday services, but we have really neglected the "from house to house" part of this work. We have to do a better job at this. We must, as the song says, "ring the message out."

As I have suggested elsewhere, why not take a whole year and work to convert one single person? Just one lost soul (we all surely know lots more than that). Become friends with them, spend time together, have them to your home for a meal, and over time, their hearts will grow open and more receptive to the word of God. When the time feels right, invite them to a service, a guest speaker series the church is conducting, your home for a one-hour Bible study, or the Vacation Bible School the church has decided to start. Take a whole year and work on one lost soul. If everyone in the church worked to save one soul, the church would double every year. That demonstrates the power of working together, with each member doing what they can do, to accomplish great things for God. "Now to Him who is able to do exceedingly abundantly above all that we ask or think, according to the power that works in us, to Him be glory in the church by Christ Jesus to all generations, forever and ever. Amen" (Ephesians 3:20-21).

3. As Ephesians 3:20 reminds us, God's power can work through the church. God can empower us (just us normal, regular, every day folks) to do His will. We are not left on our own to struggle to do things all by ourselves; we are strengthened and enabled by God, who will work in us and through us. "For it is God who works in you both to will and to do for His good pleasure" (Philippians 2:13). We are all familiar with Philippians 4:13 – "I can do all things through Christ who strengthens me." God can do all things; His power will work in us if we do our part.

Our preaching must be from the Book (2 Timothy 4:2 – "preach the word"). Gimmicks, games, and other forms of entertainment are not God's way. We cannot convert people with anything but the Bible, and we cannot grow to spiritual maturity without the word of God. The word of God, combined with the fervent prayers of godly people (James 5:16), will empower us to do all God wants us to do.

When people visit our services, we must try our best to make them feel comfortable and welcome. We have to be genuinely glad they have come and do all we can to show them our appreciation for the time and effort it takes to visit some new place. (It helps if they have children who also attend, for our children to make them feel welcome as well.) Nobody should be made to feel unwelcome when they attend our worship services or Bible classes.

4. We also must be united in purpose (1 Corinthians 1:10-13). We are the family of God. We are all on the same team. It doesn't matter how different we may be in our secular work or financial status, in our race or skin color, in our politics, or in our opinions about the current issues of the day; in Christ, we are all to be one family.

Two identifying marks of true New Testament Christianity are love (John 13:34-35) and unity (John 17:20-23). Others will see love or a lack of it. They will see that we are united or divided. They will see if we work together or run off those who may be from a background different than ours. Many churches are torn apart by discord—some over personality differences, often over doctrinal matters, and some with improper attitudes. Unity and harmony must prevail if we want to be the Lord's people in the twenty-first century. As Ephesians 4:1-3 emphasizes, "endeavoring to keep the unity of the Spirit in the bond of peace."

5. Finally, those who make up the local church must be willing to pay the price of being a Jesus follower. Christianity demands sacrifice (Luke 9:57-62; 14:28-30).

It will take time. Bible studies with the lost, visiting the weak, the unfaithful, the sick, the shut-in, and visitors to our services all take time. These things don't happen by accident, on their own. We must be intentional in giving time to be New Testament Christians.

We must use and develop our talents. Get involved. Do your part. Figure out what you can do that you aren't doing right now. Maybe take the next year and plan to do something that you have never done before. It won't be easy at first, but it will get easier as time goes on.

It will also take some money to pay for the things the church needs to do. Supporting preachers in the local church and around the world requires money in the treasury, given on the first day of the week to the work of the Lord (see Day 30 again). Newspaper articles, tracts, Bible correspondence courses, radio and TV work, and Bible class material for our studies will all cost money.

We must be careful not to develop a country-club mentality about the church. Many people, even Christians, seem to think that the church exists to meet their needs and to make them happy, and everyone just needs to do what they want. The church is designed by God to meet the spiritual needs of people and to glorify God through worship and service. Far too many selfish people want to run things their own way, getting back to human wisdom rather than being satisfied to do things God's way.

NOTES

DAY 34

Planting New Churches

In addition to the things we talked about on Day 27—two smaller churches merging into one congregation for additional strength and unity—there are times when it is appropriate for a church to send some of its members to another place to start a new, faithful church. Even though it will be small at first, the new church can often have great potential for growth and for glorifying God by expanding the borders of the kingdom.

There are many towns, villages, cities, and counties across America (and in other parts of the world as well) that do not contain one faithful church. Those people need the gospel as much as anyone else. If we don't take the gospel to them, how will they hear (without a preacher—Romans 10:14)? Jesus told us in the Great Commission to "go" to those places—remember Matthew 28:19-20 and Mark 16:15-16?

Do you recall from grammar classes in grade school that a verb is a word of action? The first verb in the Great Commission is the imperative action word, "go." The action required by this assignment is to get out of our church buildings, out of our homes, out of our soft recliners, out of our comfort zones, and go to where lost people are, in an effort to save them. All too often, churches construct a nice meeting house, put up a sign with the times of their services, and then sit back and expect lost people to come to them. "We have the truth, it's free to everyone, and all they have to do is come and we'll teach them. If they really want to be saved, all they have to do is ask."

The only problem is that the Great Commission doesn't tell lost people to come; it tells saved people to go. It is much easier to stay than to go. We are more comfortable staying than going—in our seats, in our houses, in our church buildings, in our pews, in our not caring attitude about people who are lost. It's true that every once in a while, someone happens to wander into our services. Maybe they saw our website on the internet, or maybe they just drove by on the street and saw the sign and somehow found their way to our building at the right time to attend a service. That's like going fishing and having a fish jump in your boat. It doesn't happen very often.

Strengthening the Local Church

What the Great Commission requires is for us to go and take the gospel to the lost multitudes around us. It's fine for us to invite people to our services. "Come and see" is often a good opening line for beginning the process of teaching the lost (see Day 8). We need to do more of that. But it isn't going to happen accidentally. When we have a special service (or any service, for that matter), we need to go out and invite our neighbors, relatives, friends, co-workers, fellow students, and anyone else we can reach. Most of them will probably be people who live near us or work where we do.

For those of us who are Christians, who understand the importance of the Bible, the church, assemblies, and Bible studies, we realize that it is imperative for us to go where those things take place, even if it is a substantial drive from our home. But for non-Christians who live further away from our meeting place, it will be rare for a person to drive many miles for something they aren't even sure they need. We have likely all known Christians whose job took them to a place where the nearest faithful church was a long way off. Some Christians may drive as far as two or even three hours to be with brothers and sisters in the Lord. But non-Christians are just not likely to even consider doing something like that, are they? I applaud the faith of those disciples who make such sacrifices to serve the Master, but we just can't expect unbelievers to do the same.

So there are many locations around our country and the world that need some people of faith to reach out with confidence and trust in God and start a small, new group. Here are some suggestions about things that might help in this type of work for God.

Understand that you will likely start with a small core group (probably 12 or less in many cases). Everyone will have to pitch in and do what they can to meet all the needs of this group of Christians. The same person may have to teach a class, lead a prayer, pass the Lord's Supper, and then shake everyone's hand on the way out, often all in the same service. (Oh, and they may have to lead singing also, even if they don't think they can sing.) Hopefully, it won't be that way at every service, but then again, it might be.

If the group starts with a preacher at all, he might have to get another outside job to pay the bills because the church will not be able to pay him a full-time salary at first, and it is often hard to get enough outside support to take care of everything. So it will be challenging for him to work all week, then preach the sermons, and maybe teach a Bible class every week. But this work can be rewarding, and God will notice the sacrifice (Hebrews 6:10; 1 Corinthians 15:58). In these times we live in, if a man can get a decent secular job to help with his preaching efforts, one big benefit from this will be that he can have better health insurance options through his secular job. But if more men are willing to do this, we might be able to start more new churches and do it faster.

I grew up in Southern Illinois and know most of the congregations around Southern and Central Illinois. They are composed of good, honest people who work hard at their jobs, love the Lord, and want to do right. Most of the churches in that area are fairly small and often go through cycles of growth and decline. A few have merged with other churches in the area from time to time as they have become smaller over the years through deaths and people moving away. But there are quite a few small to mid-size communities that do not have one faithful church. I could probably sit down and name about 10-12 small cities (or towns) in Illinois that need a church of Jesus Christ. Again, most of them have a church where members can drive within an hour or so, and while the Christians are willing to do that, wouldn't it be nice if they didn't have to? But we aren't really talking about a more convenient situation for those who are already Christians; we are talking about saving their lost friends and neighbors who will not drive that hour with them to learn the truth.

To make this work in many cases, the group will probably need to meet at a home (or homes) in the beginning. Many churches have started this way. With real estate costs going up all the time, it only makes sense to utilize our homes in a greater way than (perhaps) we have before. You can use your home for Bible studies (with Christians, non-Christians, or both), hospitality, singings, studies for young people, prayer times. There are multiple references in the New Testament to first-century churches that met in people's homes (Acts 20:20; Romans 16:3-5, 23; 1 Corinthians 16:19; Philemon 1-2). When the church grows, you may then consider renting a larger facility of some kind. The possibilities are endless. Start small, but dream big (Psalm 126:1-3).

So, if you live in an area where there is no faithful church nearby, can you put together 6-12 fired-up Christians who are willing to accept the challenge and start a new congregation where none currently meet? Can you project confidence and enthusiasm into the group? Can you trust in the promise of Jesus, who, after telling the apostles to take the gospel everywhere, assured them, "I am with you always, even to the end of the age?" Do you believe He will be with you also?

NOTES

DAY 35

Mobilizing the Local Church

I hope you are enjoying and profiting spiritually from this series of discussions on *Strengthening the Local Church*. I truly pray that they are being helpful to you. For the next few days, I want to focus on the value of several groups in the church, people who can use their talents to help the church grow spiritually and numerically.

There seems to be a feeling on the part of way too many Christians that, if they can't ever serve as a preacher, elder, or deacon, they really aren't very important to the Lord and His work. That is most unfortunate, because the Bible teaches that God loves every person, without partiality or favoritism (Acts 10:34-35; Romans 2:11; James 2:1-4). Every person, male or female, is important to the Lord and vital to accomplishing His will in the world.

Each of us is a unique individual, created in God's image, with an immortal soul, and intended to glorify Him while living on the earth. You know people I may never know. You love people I have never even met. You have, within your realm of influence, people who need to be saved and who may have been placed in your life by God, so that you can touch them with the gospel. If you don't do that, it may well be that no one else ever will either. And that is true for me also. It is true for all of us who are Jesus followers.

Two passages make it abundantly clear that everyone who is a disciple of Christ is important to His work.

1 Corinthians 12:12-31 compares the church to a physical body and teaches us that every part of the body is important to its proper functioning. No one should feel more important than anyone else, as we perform our work for Him. No one should feel inferior to others, either. We all matter to God.

The context of this passage concerns the spiritual gifts that first-century Christians received before the New Testament was completed. Some thought themselves better than others because of their gift, and some didn't think they were as important as others because they got a different gift than someone else. But they were all to work together, just as all the various parts of our bodies work together. Although we do not have these same miraculous gifts today, we are all gifted by God with natural talents and abilities that should be used to help other people come closer to God and to glorify Him in every way we can. And Paul points out that, even with the miraculous aspects of their gifts, the greatest gift of all is to love others.

Romans 12 is an entire chapter of the New Testament that emphasizes how we are different, but that we should all use our abilities in a way that honors the Giver. You can do things I cannot, and you are accountable to God for do what you can do. Likewise, I need to do whatever I can and am accountable for it.

Nothing is easy the first time you try it. It takes practice to learn how to do certain things, like ride a bicycle, hit a good backhand in tennis, lead singing in the church, teach a Bible class, or deliver a sermon from God's word that will stir up and build up fellow Christians. Medical students practice in multiple situations before they begin performing surgery, pulling a tooth, or doing a root canal. Airplane pilots and new automobile drivers have to have a certain number of practice hours with a trained instructor before they do those things on their own.

But first, they have to identify what they want to do. In the church, I am not certain we encourage one another enough to learn how to do new things for God that we have never done before. A persistent elder in Illinois called me every Sunday morning for several weeks before I agreed to try to lead one song before the Bible study class. If he had quit asking me, I might have never done it at all. We should think about things we can (or might be able to) do for God. And we have to be willing to stretch ourselves and try something we have never done before. The first time will likely not be great. But we might be better than we realize and able to do more things than we dream.

Perhaps this is the best place to mention again what is often referred to as the 80/20 rule. Basically, this most unfortunate truth states that in most organizations, 80% of the work is done by 20% of the people. We need everyone to pitch in and do the work they are qualified to do. The key to success is to change that statistic by having every member (100%) do all they can. Can you be counted on? Think about it.

Please consider one more verse that speaks to this subject. "(Christ), from whom the whole body, joined and knit together by what every joint supplies, according to the effective working by which every part does its share, causes growth of the body for the edifying of itself in love" (Ephesians 4:16). This is part of a larger context (verses 11-16). It might be helpful for you to read all of those verses right now. While all of the text is important, let's focus on a couple of vital lessons from verse 16.

Notice that he is speaking about the spiritual (and perhaps numerical) growth of the local church. He uses the significant word edifying in this passage. It refers to the building up of the body of Christ. God never intended the church to languish, dry up, or die on the vine. He designed it to be dynamic, alive, moving forward toward godliness.

The key to that type of dynamic growth is that the church is to be "joined and knit together by what every joint supplies." Everyone is important to God and should be regarded as important to the other members of the church. We all have talents and abilities, and something we can add to the Lord's work. There were no "no talent" people in the parable of Jesus (Matthew 25:14-30). Some may only have one talent, but they should use it to the full glory of Almighty God, who gave them that talent in the first place. If they bury that one talent, nobody will benefit from it. We need everyone doing everything they can to God's glory.

The second important phrase here is "every part does its share." That again shows us that we all have a part or a share in the Lord's work. Our work may differ from that of another Christian, but that's the way God designed the church to function, with everyone doing what they can.

Two of my nieces, Laura and Lindsey, years ago, gave me a little plaque for my office which says, "What we are is God's gift to us; what we become is our gift to God." Does that say something to your heart? I hope it does.

I want to spend the next several days discussing what various groups of Christians can do that will strengthen the church where they worship. The groups I will discuss are single Christians, older Christians, women, and teens/young people. May the Lord richly bless you as you seek to do His will.

NOTES

DAY 36

Mobilizing the Local Church: Single Christians

Many churches have a significant percentage of their members who are single. Excluding children, many of the adult members are not married. There are a number of reasons for this growing demographic in the Lord's church.

- Human lifespan is longer – there are more widows and widowers.
- The divorce rate is higher – sometimes even among Christians.
- Many never marry – some are unasked; some are unanswered. And a higher percentage than ever decides not to marry, or else they are waiting until later in life to marry.

I realize that this can be very discouraging to some who fall into this category and who would love to be married if the right situation would arise. Some are content in being single and have made a conscious decision not to marry.

But I am afraid that there are too many single Christians who feel they cannot serve the Lord effectively because they are single, and as a result, a powerful spiritual force is left untapped in many congregations.

There are many positive and valuable things that a single Christian can do. I would like to remind you of some of those things in the hopes that we can mobilize a group of disciples who can make a huge difference in the life of a church in the here and now and a great difference in other people's eternal destiny.

1) Do not become discouraged.
   Being single is no reason to have low self-esteem. Singles sometimes ask, "What's wrong with me?" Nothing is wrong with you, except perhaps that you are focusing on the wrong thing. Look to your strengths, talents, and abilities. (Married people who concentrate only on what they can't do or don't have will never be happy either.)

   There are many great men and women of God in the Bible who were single (either never having married or having lost a spouse). In the Old Testament, some of them were Elijah, Daniel, Jeremiah, Ezekiel, and Mordecai. In the New Testament, we have Paul, Mary, Martha, Lazarus, John the Baptist, Timothy, Barnabas, and of course, Jesus.

When you find yourself feeling lonely, do something for someone else to take the focus off of your aloneness. Visit with friends, enjoy the children of others (buy them things; take them places you would like to go, like the zoo or a museum). Just keep busy doing something.

2) Recognize your opportunities.
The apostle Paul, in 1 Corinthians 7:7-8, recommends the single life. He is not forbidding people from getting married (1 Timothy 4:3), but he wants you to realize that you are definitely not a second-class Christian if you are unmarried.

The fact is that marriage divides a person's interests into two areas —serving the Lord and being with your mate. An unmarried person has the time to do things for God that married people often cannot do. Notice this passage from 1 Corinthians 7:32-35: "But I want you to be without care. He who is unmarried cares for the things of the Lord – how he may please the Lord. But he who is married cares about the things of the world – how he may please his wife. There is a difference between a wife and a virgin. The unmarried woman cares about the things of the Lord, that she may be holy both in body and in spirit. But she who is married cares about the things of the world – how she may please her husband. And this I say for your own profit, not that I may put a leash on you, but for what is proper, and that you may serve the Lord without distraction."

He continues on to discuss one who does not give his daughter in marriage and says that such a one has chosen what is better. There are some advantages to being single over being married. (There are also advantages in being married over being single. It is not all one-sided in either direction.)

Some advantages a single Christian has are:
- Can be more spontaneous
- Freer to come and go
- No one to answer to about time
- More time to study the Bible and pray
- Have get-togethers at your place (make it a potluck)
- More time to attend gospel meetings in other places

- Often in a position to contribute more than average to the church
- Galatians 6:10

3) Maintain sexual purity.
   This is very important. A single Christian must work very hard, with the Lord's help, to keep himself/herself pure.

   There are two important things to watch out for—your friends (1 Corinthians 15:33) and your activities (Ephesians 5:11).

   Remember that you are the salt of the earth and the light of the world (Matthew 5:13-16). Don't let your unmarried status be an excuse to sin it up. Think about the example you are setting for others.

4) Help others.
   One of the biggest problems for single Christians is turning inward, only being concerned with self. Give of yourself to others (Acts 20:33-35; Matthew 20:25-28).

   Matthew 19:10-12 speaks of those who refuse marriage ("make themselves eunuchs") for "the kingdom of heaven's sake." Being single often gives you more time to help others.
   - The needy – James 1:27
   - Sick, hungry, lonely people – Matthew 25:31-46
   - Spiritually weak – Galatians 6:1-2
   - The lost – Matthew 4:19

Conclusion
If you find yourself in this situation, by choice or by circumstance, use it to the glory of God. The church has a huge army of single, godly men and women out there who need to be mobilized in His service. Realize that this is an opportunity to serve God and the church and the world around you in a way that will make a difference in the lives and eternity of others. May God richly bless you.

NOTES

DAY 37

Mobilizing the Local Church: Women

Feel free to disagree, but I do not believe it is an overstatement to say that, in many congregations, the women are stronger spiritually than the men. I am convinced that women are perhaps the single most important force in the church. We naturally spend time discussing scriptural limitations on women, placed there by God Himself, things that women cannot do. But most of those things are public functions, while the vast majority of our work for God is done outside the assemblies, behind the scenes, unheralded, often unnoticed (except by God).

Both Galatians 3:26-28 and 1 Peter 3:7 refer to the unity of the church ("neither male nor female; for you are all one in Christ Jesus") and the equality of men and women in the sight of God ("heirs together of the grace of life"). That doesn't mean we have been given the same public roles in the church. Passages like 1 Timothy 2:11-15 and 1 Corinthians 14:33-35 do limit some of the things that women can do in the assemblies of the church. The qualifications for those who would serve as elders and deacons require them to be "the husband of one wife" (1 Timothy 3:1-13), which excludes women from serving in those official positions, in spite of what our modern American culture likes or doesn't like. That is not going to change what God says. And, in the controversial passage about a woman's head covering, God states, through the Holy Spirit, then through the apostle Paul, "But I want you to know that the head of every man is Christ, the head of woman is man, and the head of Christ is God" (1 Corinthians 11:3).

But what a blessing godly women are to the Lord's church. Many of us got our earliest Bible teaching, after our mothers, from a good woman who taught us how to love God (in many cases, like my own, our mothers were also our teachers at the church). When we reach a certain age (whatever it might be), most of us start having male teachers, but by that time, we usually have a fairly good working knowledge of the Bible, how it all fits together, and what it means for our lives and eternity. Those wonderful women helped us to form our spiritual personality, so to speak, and we will be forever grateful (literally, forever).

I am probably not the only one who sees himself in the story of Timothy, Eunice, and Lois (see Acts 16:1-5; 2 Timothy 1:3-5 and 2 Timothy

3:14-17). I am the weak link in that story because I do not deserve to be compared to Timothy, but my mother and grandmother, like his, taught me the scriptures from my youth, without the help of my father. He obeyed the gospel when I was a Senior in High School (also due to my mother's influence), later became an elder, and did some preaching for the local church where our family worshiped. But before that, my love for God had been instilled in me by my mother and grandmother. My mother-in-law and her mother did the same thing for my wife. It is somewhat frightening to think about where we and our children would be spiritually if not for the influence of our mothers. They were not perfect, of course, but they helped chart the course for our whole lives with their godly examples. My guess is that literally millions of souls will be in heaven eternally because their mothers kept the faith without help from a Christian husband and instilled those values in their sons and daughters.

So, in almost every case, churches have a greater impact on the world and their communities because of the good things done by godly women in the Lord's church. Occasionally you hear a story of a godly man whose wife was not a Christian and who successfully reared and trained his children without the help of his wife, but you hear many more stories that are the other way around, a good woman with a man who was not a spiritual helper in bringing up their children to love and serve God. While there are some restrictions that God has placed on what women can do in a local church, there are many things that they are still allowed to do in offering their lives as a spiritual sacrifice (Romans 12:1-2).

Most women are great encouragers of others. Most of them are naturally gifted in this area, and many have sharpened their skills by rearing their own children. You can see this trait exemplified in the happy, smiling faces of the children as they come out of Bible class and return to their parents. It is obvious they have enjoyed the learning experience the teacher has provided for them.

Women may also be teachers of others, not simply children. Older women are instructed to teach and help younger women become people of faith, morality, and dignity (Titus 2:3-5). And the added value of teaching biblical principles comes as the younger women realize that this is not just the teaching of facts, but the imparting of a way of life. They can see, in the personal life of the older woman teaching them, that she both believes and practices these spiritual truths. They are guiding principles for how a Christian woman lives every day, not just on Sunday mornings. As Paul says to Titus, these women are "teachers of good things" (verse 3). As Paul emphasizes in 1 Timothy 2:15, through giving birth and teaching these values to young people, they help them to "continue in faith, love, and holiness, with self-control."

And, as we noted from the example of Lois, this godliness can also be transmitted to grandchildren. There have been many people who have ignored the teaching from their own parents, but those same men and women have continued to seek to influence their grandchildren and great-grandchildren. Never give up on your family while there is still hope. It is great when children and grandchildren get good teaching at church, but don't expect those classes to do it all: the church and the home need to work together to instill these values in our young people.

Women can also teach men in private situations, like Aquila and Priscilla did in Acts 18:24-28. Paul referred to this husband and wife team as "my fellow workers" in Romans 16:3. They were not assistants, second-class teachers, or underlings. They worked together to help Apollos come to a deeper understanding of God's will.

Women also have the opportunity to teach their friends who don't know the Lord. It might be through a regular Bible study in the home on a specific morning, afternoon, or evening each week. They can also be a good influence by inviting the friends, neighbors, or other family members to attend a meeting, service, or maybe a Vacation Bible School, along with their children. The bottom line is that women can teach in any situation that does not involve taking authority over a man (1 Timothy 2:12). We need to realize that there are many more opportunities for a woman to teach others than there are situations in which she cannot.

There is a reason why elders and deacons are to be married. God said, in the beginning of the world, that it is not good for man to be alone. The woman makes the man's life full and complete, and God created her to provide strength, support, and encouragement for the man (Genesis 2:18; 1 Corinthians 11:8-9). Most women are not concerned about getting credit or making headlines, and most do not feel in competition with others (many men do feel a competitive spirit). Elders, deacons, and preachers can all benefit from a supportive wife who appreciates their efforts to serve God and help others make it to heaven.

Women are also in a position to help others in need—the lonely, the sick, those in hospitals and nursing homes (like Dorcas in Acts 9:36-42), Phoebe (Romans 16:1-2), and others who have the opportunity to make a difference in people's lives and their eternity (Galatians 6:10).

NOTES

DAY 38

Mobilizing the Local Church: Young Christians

Young people play an important role in the spiritual life of a local church. In the Bible, there are many references to young people and their significant role in God's plan.

- Timothy was a young preacher for whom Paul had a special place in his heart and in his work.

- Titus was also a young evangelist that Paul worked with and encouraged (at least, he was younger than Paul, who referred to him as a "son in the faith").

- John Mark is believed to be the young man who fled when Christ was arrested (Mark 15:51-52). Later, he wrote the book of Mark in the New Testament.

- Many Bible scholars believe it is possible that Mary, the mother of Jesus, was a teenager when the angel told her she would bring God's Son into the world.

- Joseph was only 17 years old when his brothers sold him into slavery, beginning his journey toward a life of serving God.

- Jeremiah referred to himself as "a youth" (Jeremiah 1:6). He felt inadequate to his task, but God trusted him to do the work and be faithful.

- Much of the book of Proverbs was written as advice from an older, experienced person to a younger one struggling with difficult challenges in life.

- And there are other examples, as well.

The primary responsibility for rearing children in the Lord belongs to the parents, especially the father. "And you fathers, do not provoke your children to wrath, but bring them up in the training and admonition of the Lord" (Ephesians 6:4). But there is no reason why the family and the church cannot work together as partners in helping young men and women grow and mature in the faith.

Parents need to plan spiritual activities for their children to train them to love and serve God. It will obviously be helpful to take them to the classes and services of the church, and to visit other faithful congregations during special times of Bible study and sermons. Often, the key to success in a young person's Bible class is not the teacher during a 40-minute study period, but rather the parents who make sure the child is prepared and has studied well before they come to class. If teenagers, for example, do not have their lessons prepared for class time, that is as much a parent problem as a young person's issue.

Bible classes at the church building should supplement, not replace, the Bible studies the family is doing together at home. But because many children are not receiving any, or very little, Bible teaching at home, it is vital for the church to have a great Bible class curriculum set up to make certain that young people are learning as much of God's word as possible, in an organized and helpful arrangement.

One of our goals in Bible classes must be to not only teach Bible facts to young people, and that is very important, but we must also teach these tender hearts to love the Lord. Teachers must stress the application of Bible teaching to the young person's life and show them how following the Bible will lead to a happier, more successful life as well as to an eternal reward. Churches must do their best to choose teachers who do not simply relay Bible truth to young people, but whose lives also match the message. That was one of Christ's criticisms of the first-century Pharisees: "they say, and do not do." Our lives must be living illustrations of how Jesus can change our lives for the better, and they should really emphasize that He should make a difference in how we do everything, not just "church things."

A book published in 2009, entitled *Already Gone*, makes a strong case for teaching Biblical evidences to young people. It claims that many young folks make the decision to leave the Lord in late elementary or middle school, rather than high school or college. Mentally, they have checked out long before they possess the freedom to act on that decision, and we only realize it when they go away to college and immediately quit serving God. In reality, they quit in their hearts long ago.

So we must emphasize why they should believe in God, why they must believe that Jesus is His Son, and why it is consistent to trust that the Bible is a special book, breathed out by God for man's eternal guidance and direction.

Elders, preachers, teachers, and other faithful Christians need to realize that many of the children we see regularly at services are not getting the father-and-mother example they need to be well-rounded in their faith. If you know of young people whose father is not a godly example, try to help the mother and the child by providing an excellent example of a righteous man who shows an interest in helping others to mature in Christ. If the mother is lacking in her influence, other godly women should make it a special point to encourage her children to be faithful to God. Many of us were encouraged by an older Christian, to whom we were not necessarily related, who took an interest in us and spent time helping us to learn to love Christ.

Some parents have expressed remorse over having lost their children because they didn't place enough priority on spiritual things while their children were growing up. We don't get a second chance to do a better job at that, but we can perhaps make a difference for our grandchildren or for the children of other Christians whom we can influence in a godly way.

It has been said that children are the church of tomorrow, and there is certainly truth in that statement. But we can't wait until they are grown to try to instill in them the value of serving God. We must start now. Training classes for both boys and girls can show them some of the things that they should be working toward as they mature. Let young boys do what they can in the worship services. Give them some instructions on how to lead singing, lead a public prayer, give a short talk from the Bible, or how to serve the Lord's Supper.

Many religious groups have, for years, engaged in fun and games and food and have turned to many other unscriptural forms of entertainment in an attempt to excite the young and keep them coming to planned activities. It is not the responsibility of the church to provide entertainment to try to keep young people interested in God. Entertainment is fine, in its place, which is to say, when it is provided by the home and family, not by the church. Families do need to provide such opportunities for their children. Those who do not will regret it later. But do not involve the church in things that are not a part of the God-given mission of the church.

The older Christians can add much in the way of experience, wisdom, and understanding of the Bible to ensure that young people do not express "zeal without knowledge" (Romans 10:1-2). We need each other. So let's do what we can to help our young people love and obey God, starting when they are still young (Ecclesiastes 12:1).

NOTES

DAY 39

Mobilizing the Local Church: Older Christians

We are all growing older. I have lived long enough to realize the truth I had been told about for most of my life is very real. Time really does seem to go by faster as you get older. I saw a t-shirt advertised online the other day that summed it all up very well. It said, "I thought growing old would take longer." All I can say is, Amen!

However young or old you may be (chronologically or spiritually), God wants us all to grow stronger and do all we can to serve Him, no matter our biological age. In 1 John 2:12-14, the apostle speaks of the various stages of life when he refers to little children (those who are very young), young men (those somewhere in the middle), and fathers (those who are older and, hopefully, more mature in the Lord). His point is that the older one is and the longer he (or she) has been a Christian, the greater, stronger, more spiritually developed, and more service-oriented that person should be.

"The silver-haired head is a crown of glory, If it is found in the way of righteousness" (Proverbs 16:31). The "if" in that verse shows us that getting older does not always or automatically mean getting better, but it should.

The phrase," silver-haired head," speaks of a long life of devotion to God. There are so many examples of older saints who faithfully obeyed the will of God for their entire lives. We are pointed to Simeon (Luke 2:25-29), Anna (Luke 2:36-38), and Paul the aged (Philemon 9), and we are encouraged to imitate their godly examples (1 Corinthians 11:1). There is a dignity and grace that surrounds an older Christian. In addition to the multiple Bible characters mentioned already (and lots of others, as well), we have all known people in our own life experiences who have symbolized the attitude of faithfully serving God with all their heart, soul, mind, and strength for all the days they lived. We should always be grateful to God for their influence in our lives.

With age comes years of experience that have helped to shape and mold them into what they have become. Older Christians have usually had many experiences in life that younger people could not have had, just because they have lived longer. Hebrews 5:12-14 speaks of the fact that, because of the length of time that they had been serving God, they should have grown, simply by what the writer calls, "by reason of use." They have experienced so many things (often both good and bad) that the next generation has not (yet), and we can learn from and be affected by their endurance and steadfastness.

Perhaps that is why church leaders are so often referred to as "elders" in the New Testament. One of the biblical qualifications that an elder must meet is "not a novice." Paul adds that this will help to keep him from being puffed up with pride. These men have learned many valuable life lessons through their varied experiences. It is a fact that the more you learn, the more you realize how little you know. It has been said that you learn to make good decisions through experience and that you gain experience by making bad decisions. It is probably also true that you can gain experience at times by making the right decisions and seeing how God blesses those choices.

Older Christians should be worthy of the respect of all of us. The Bible teaches us this over and over.

"You shall rise before the gray headed and honor the presence of an old man, and fear your God: I am the LORD" (Leviticus 19:32).

"Do not rebuke an older man, but exhort him as a father, younger men as brothers, older women as mothers, younger women as sisters, with all purity" (1 Timothy 5:1-2).

"Likewise you younger people, submit yourselves to your elders. Yes, all of you be submissive to one another, and be clothed with humility, for God resists the proud, But gives grace to the humble" (1 Peter 5:5). One of society's greatest failures is the lack of respect shown to older people these days. Let's make certain that we are not guilty in the Lord's church.

Older disciples, in most cases, have a greater sense of eternity than those who are younger. They have a big-picture view of life that helps them to prioritize the spiritual over the temporal (or temporary; see 2 Corinthians 4:16-18). That's why Paul could write, in his final letter in the New Testament, "For I am already being poured out as a drink offering, and the time of my departure is at hand. I have fought the good fight, I have finished the race, I have kept the faith. Finally, there is laid up for me the crown of righteousness, which the Lord, the righteous judge, will give to me on that Day, and not to me only but also to all who have loved His appearing" (2 Timothy 4:6-8). Anyone could die at any time, but those who are older are much closer to death, in many cases, than those who are younger. They also have more time to think about death and the need to be prepared for it.

Solomon summed much of this up for us in Proverbs 20:29: "The glory of young men is their strength, And the splendor of old men is their gray head." A balance is needed here. Young people bring strength, zeal, enthusiasm, and excitement to the church. The older people bring wisdom, experience, greater Bible knowledge, and a deeper spiritual and eternal perspective to what we do together. Both of those viewpoints are vital and important to the work of a local church. We need each other. The point of this message is that the church needs older members. (It needs younger ones also, but that point has already been made in other places.) There should be no generation gap, and there will not be if both the old and the young have the proper attitude toward each other. This is a two-way street; each age group should love and appreciate the value of the other.

In too many places, the young tend to disdain and devalue the older. They think the old people don't know anything, while, in most cases, they may not want to follow a certain path or decision because they did it when they were younger and learned that it doesn't work. On the other hand, some elderly people do not deserve the respect of the young because they only grumble, complain, and find fault with younger Christians and think they are all uninformed and foolish. Maybe they are, but maybe they are not also. Judge ideas based on their own merit, not on the age of the one who suggested something they thought might help the Lord's work, whether young or old.

Job stated in Job 12:12-13, "Wisdom is with aged men, And with length of days, understanding. With Him (that's God, rh) are wisdom and strength, He has counsel and understanding." Wisdom usually comes through both knowledge and experience. The elderly do not always have all the answers, but they often have gone through situations and experiences that provide them with valuable insight that should not be automatically ignored, just because they are older. It is said that hindsight has 20/20 vision. Often, this can help the young avoid some of the mistakes and pitfalls of life (see Proverbs 9:9 and 12:15). We discard the old at our own peril.

We can learn from the past, but we can only live in the present. Sometimes we dwell on "the good ole' days" because we have forgotten the problems they brought us. We tend to remember only the good. We need the older Christians; they have much to offer the Lord's work. If you are older, don't retire from God's service. Keep working for Him in whatever time you have. The Lord's people need you.

NOTES

DAY 40

One Generation Away

I have heard it said all of my life that the church is just one generation away from apostasy. And I believe that to be true. After all, that's the pattern we see repeated over and over in the Old Testament book of Judges. Faithful during the lifetime of the judge, shortly after the judge's death, Israel would forsake God and get involved in sin. After a period of time had lapsed and the people finally repented, God would raise up another judge, and the cycle would be repeated.

The same principle applies today. If we fail to stand up for truth, it will not take long for error to dominate. If we don't teach our children and ground them in a full knowledge of God's will, they will easily fall victim to the deceitful schemes of the devil and be led astray.

But is that the only way to look at it? Wouldn't the opposite also be a possibility? Wouldn't it also be true that we are only one generation away from spreading the gospel to the whole world? Do you also believe that it is possible?

After all, the first century church accomplished this goal as commanded by Jesus in the Great Commission (Matthew 28:19-20; Mark 16:15-16) and also found in Acts 1:8. And Jesus gave this huge assignment to only eleven disciples! Can you even imagine how inadequate that must have made them feel? How could they possibly complete a job like that?

But Colossians 1:23 tells us that they did it. "If indeed you continue in the faith, grounded and steadfast, and are not moved away from the hope of the gospel which you heard, which was preached to every creature under heaven, of which I, Paul, became a minister."

If Jesus gave the Great Commission in A.D. 30 and Paul wrote Colossians around A.D. 60-63, they accomplished the task in about 30 years, approximately one generation.

Couldn't we do it if we really set our hearts to it?

Strengthening the Local Church

I understand that there are a lot more people in the world now, compared to the world population in the first century. But, we are starting with a lot more than eleven disciples, aren't we? And don't we have the advantages of speed, travel, mass communications, computers, and many other tools that they did not have? If they could succeed, why, so far, haven't we?

Another principle I have heard repeatedly during my lifetime is this: If we continue doing what we've always done in the same way we've always done it, we will get the same results. As much as we may hate to admit it, that's true, too, isn't it?

Let me suggest three things that I think will help.

1) Quit fighting so much among ourselves.
    I know we are to contend for the faith (Jude 3) and fight the good fight of faith (1 Timothy 6:12). I know there are false teachers whose doctrines will destroy souls (2 Peter 2). I know time needs to be spent to combat these destructive heresies.

    So argue and debate when you feel you must. But do not get so caught up in trying to find fault with your brothers and sisters that you forget about the lost souls who live within your sphere of influence.

    I am not arguing that it's wrong to argue. All I'm suggesting is that we not spend all of our time fighting each other. Try to win some lost souls as well.

2) Have a greater sense of urgency.
    Jesus was never in a hurry. He never rushed to try to accomplish something before it was time. But He also felt a sense of urgency that compelled Him to accomplish what He could while He had the opportunity. "I must work the works of Him who sent Me while it is day; the night is coming when no one can work" (John 9:4).

    No one knows how much time we have before the Lord returns. But, someday, God's longsuffering will end and the Judgment Day will occur. "If you live every day as though it is your last, someday you'll be right."

    Paul said it this way, "And do this, knowing the time, that now it is high time to awake out of sleep; for now our salvation is nearer than when we first believed. The night is far spent, the day is at hand. Therefore let us cast off the works of darkness, and let us put on the armor of light" (Romans 13:11-12).

3) Work harder.
We just have to be more diligent. We have to stop passing up so many opportunities (James 4:17).

Do we have some among us who are in a position to move to other countries where the pure gospel has not been preached for many years and plant faithful churches that will convert hundreds, and perhaps thousands, of lost souls? Are there those who are willing to sacrifice to move to these hard, unevangelized areas of the world?

And for those who cannot move elsewhere, are you willing to work harder and be more concerned about all of the lost souls around you? Can you do more? Will you do more? Will I do more?

Conclusion
There are several hundred thousand Christians in non-institutional, conservative churches of Christ today. Eleven disciples evangelized their world in the first century. Can our motto be "Till Jesus Comes, We'll Work?"

The only person I can change is me. "If it is to be, it is up to me." You have to decide if you want to change you. I hope you will.

We are one generation away from taking this world for Christ. Let's go out and change our world.

Biblical Insights
December 2008

NOTES

Epilogue

Thank you for reading this material. I hope you have found it encouraging and challenging as you seek to help the local church where you attend services to be stronger and more determined than ever before to obey the Lord's will.

A friend of mine is fond of saying, "If you are going to be religious, you might as well do it so it counts." His point is that there is no point in serving God if you don't really mean it. We can go through the motions and do all the right things, but if our hearts are not in the right place, it will profit us nothing. "Without faith it is impossible to please Him, for he who comes to God must believe that He is and that He is a rewarder of those who diligently seek Him" (Hebrews 11:6).

If we believe with all of our hearts that God exists and that He created the church as a place to approach Him, then we must strive to make the church all we can, from our human perspective. God has designed the church perfectly; the plan is without flaw. But those of us who make up the church are all flawed, sinful people (Romans 3:10, 23), so the way we "do" church will be imperfect.

God intended the church to be a taste of heaven on earth, and when we do our part correctly, it can be that for us. But as we fall short, the church often does not reach its full potential for helping people live closer to God.

I have attempted, in this short study, to address several key issues that I have believed for years will help the church grow, develop, be strengthened, and prosper in this sinful world we live in. There are probably other areas I should have covered, and perhaps someone more insightful than me will follow up with further teaching in those areas. Even in the things I have written about, there are, no doubt, better suggestions than the ones I have compiled, and I hope others will add those additional helpful points in their own personal circumstance.

It has become clear to me over the last number of years that leadership is perhaps the single most important area where the Lord's church needs to improve (not on God's plan, but on our execution of God's plan). No group can advance further than its leadership can take it.

Really spiritual shepherds of the people of God are needed to help us make it to heaven.

All elderships are, by nature, going to be imperfect. When the individuals are not perfect, the group and their decisions will not be perfect either. The difference lies between those who realize their imperfections and constantly strive to improve themselves and those who just accept their weaknesses. There are many really good men out there who take their job seriously and prayerfully seek to lead and guide the flock to the Promised Land. May God bless all those who are striving to make a difference in this ungodly world.

But there are also those in many churches who are unqualified to serve as elders or deacons who exert an undue and improper influence over elders, causing them to make poor decisions rather than ones that would glorify God. People flex their political muscle, through financial success or large family size or some other inappropriate means, to get their way in the church, even when it is not God's way. Some elders, not wanting to lose the financial gifts or sheer numbers of family members, give in to such pressure and hurt the cause of Christ by making decisions that may please the troublemakers but do not please God. If these ne'er-do-wells are allowed to get their way, they are actually leading the church, not the God-given elders.

People can threaten to leave the church if they don't get their way, and of course, elders don't want to lose anyone, so they often let these "influential members" hold too much sway. A godly person will not threaten to divide the people of God if they don't get their way. Division is sinful (see the "works of the flesh" in Galatians 5:19-21 and notice how many of them deal with matters of division, not unity.) Such people indeed have the freedom to state their opinion to the elders, but then they must let the elders make the final decisions for the church. And if hot-headed people leave, the church will likely be better off without them. But elders must do the godly thing in every situation and then let others make their own decisions about how they will react. It is always right to do the right thing.

Perhaps we just need more leadership training in most churches, even those that already have elders. It is a difficult, demanding job, and I am certain that the vast majority want to do the job in a helpful, biblical way.

Epilogue

The Lord's church has gone through many cycles of growth and decline, both on a local level and, even overall, in the universal church. Our job is to remain faithful, no matter what the forces of society decide around us. It is likely that, at times, things will not go well in some churches, but then, just as likely, they can be turned around and improved. We must remain ever diligent, ever true to God and His will, ever focused on pleasing God in all that we do.

This material is offered in the hope that it will help local churches to be renewed if they find themselves discouraged or broken.

When you read the Old Testament, there are multiple examples of the power of God at work in seemingly hopeless situations.

- God's people spent 430 years in bondage in Egypt and Moses led them out to the Promised Land to become a great nation.

- Many of the kings during the time of the Divided Kingdom, in both Israel and Judah, were ungodly men who rejected the things of God and served dead, empty idols. Yet, through His love and providence, God led them through that period to bring forth the Messiah.

- When even Judah was overcome by worldliness and transgression, God sent them to Babylon for seventy years before returning many of them to faithful service back in their homeland.

- The scribes and Pharisees of the first century were blessed to see and hear the Savior Himself, and yet, they rejected Him as God's chosen One.

- Through Jewish and Roman persecution and despite internal false teachers and external worldliness, the early church persevered and took the gospel to the whole world.

There are no limits to what God can do (Matthew 19:26). And He wants to use us to accomplish much for Him in our twenty-first-century world. He will not force us to do the right thing, but He will always strengthen the hearts of those who are determined to serve Him to the very end. May God bless you in your efforts to fulfill His plan, to obey His will, and to be the church of Jesus the Christ.

NOTES

Appendix Articles

Being Intentional with Your Life

That's kind of an odd title, isn't it? I hope it makes more sense as you read through the article.

By being intentional, I simply mean planning your own life and not letting others decide everything for you. I am talking about making your own decisions, based on what you know God wants you to do. Do you live your life that way?

Now, I understand that unexpected things that can occur, many of them undesirable and beyond our control. There are illnesses, deaths, problems, and trials that no one would personally choose. But even how we react to those sorts of things can be under our control.

When you are younger, you have little control over your own life. Your parents or others who are caring for you make all of your decisions for you. As you grow up, part of the maturing process is learning how to make appropriate decisions for yourself. Part of being a godly parent is training our children to make the right decisions.

As adults, we have much more control over things we do, where we go, who our friends are, and what kinds of activities we participate in. We decide what to study in school, where we will live, who we will marry, and many other important decisions of life. What kind of car will we drive, what kind of job or career will we pursue? There are many examples.

The question is, where does God fit into all of those decisions? What part does our relationship with Him play in the big things we decide about our lives? Do we make intentional decisions about what He would have us do and then act on those things?

Or are we just existing, taking whatever comes our way and having little or nothing to say about our own future?

As a Christian, a disciple of Christ, do you think about the morality of the things you do? Do you "Test all things; hold fast what is good. Abstain from every form of evil" (1 Thessalonians 5:21-22)? Do you resist the Devil so he will flee from you (James 4:7)? Do you deny yourself, take up your cross daily, and follow Him (Luke 9:23)?

It doesn't matter if you call this idea plans, hopes, dreams, vision, goals. It all amounts to the same thing: controlling your life under the influence of God's will to really make your life matter. I am talking about being proactive in living your life God's way, not merely reactive to forces around you that are out of your control.

It is said there are three types of people in the world: those who make things happen, those who watch things happen, and those who say, "What happened?" You need to make things happen with your life. Don't waste your days on earth. Be a surrendered, faithful, godly servant of Christ (1 Corinthians 15:58).

—Roger Hillis

First Century Soul Winning

When we look at the New Testament, especially the book of Acts, we see the tremendous success of first-century Christians in converting the lost. Acts 5:14 tells us: "And believers were increasingly added to the Lord, multitudes of both men and women."

Multitudes of both men and women were being saved. Multitudes. Not five or six people per year like most congregations expect these days. Multitudes. Can you try to imagine that in your mind? Is it still possible?

Let's think for a moment about how they did that.

First, they taught "publicly and from house to house" (Acts 20:20). We do pretty well with the "publicly" part. We faithfully proclaim the truth in our meetinghouses and are willing to try to convert anyone who comes to us. But how are we doing with the "from house to house" part? I fear not so well.

Second, they brought family and friends to hear the gospel. "...Now Cornelius was waiting for them, and had called together his relatives and close friends" (Acts 10:24). How much are we doing that today? How long has it been since you personally invited your relatives and close friends to hear the good news of salvation?

Third, they taught one-on-one whenever they could make such opportunities. Jesus taught Nicodemus privately (John 3). He spent time together with the Samaritan woman speaking to her of spiritual things (John 4). It appears to have been just Philip and the Ethiopian eunuch in the chariot (Acts 8). Are you bold enough and confident enough to go "one on one" with a lost person, with just a Bible between you? Can you sit across a kitchen table with a sinner and look him in the eye and teach him the plan of salvation? Have you ever done that, even once?

Fourth, they went to where the people were. Paul and Silas preached to some women who were at the riverside praying (Acts 16). Paul preached to Greek philosophers at Mars' Hill in Athens (Acts 17). On the preaching journeys, they often traveled to synagogues and schools to spread the truth (Acts 19:8-10). Again, are we doing that much?

They used these simple methods and converted multitudes. We use these methods very little, if at all, and then we shake our heads and say, "No one seems interested in the gospel anymore." What's wrong with this picture?

—Roger Hillis

Being Guest Friendly

There are several things we need to do to make certain we are sensitive to the needs of our guests. They are, after all, a great source of numerical and spiritual growth.

1. Extend a warm, friendly welcome. Do so whether the guests are on the way in or on their way out. Have you ever felt, when visiting other places, like you were basically ignored? It's a horrible feeling, and we must make sure that those who are guests at our services feel that we really were glad they came.

2. Help our guests find the appropriate Bible classes. They would like to be in the right class for their age group and spiritual level, and they also want their children to be comfortable.

3. Help the visiting family find seats together. They don't want to be separated from each other or to sit in a cramped, uncomfortable setting. If the building is full, move to the center of your row and let

our guests find room. Statistics have revealed that when a building is filled to 80% capacity, many guests feel uncomfortable and will not return. Let's make sure that doesn't happen here.

4. Be careful in Bible class about your comments and the tone with which they are offered. If you find it necessary to express disagreement with others (and, at times, this will be necessary), do so gently, not harshly. Comment on the comment, not the person.

5. We must make certain that our building and grounds are well cared for. They make an important first impression. Guests need to find a place to park close to the door. The lawn must be well-groomed. Bathrooms must be clean and odor-free. The walls should be painted, and we should be careful not to throw trash around on the floor or seats (this includes gum wrappers, etc.).

6. Song leaders need to be careful to lead songs that the congregation knows and can sing well. Our singing is really important for making a good impression with our guests and when we sing a song that we don't know well, it leaves the wrong idea in their minds. If there are unusual words or phrases in a particular song (Ebenezer, Ebon pinion, etc.), explain those terms briefly before singing the song.

7. A guest packet with information about the church would be helpful and much appreciated by those who are considering attending regularly.

8. Do not monopolize the time of the preacher and/or elders. They need to greet our guests, and many will be offended if the preacher does not even say "hello" to them. There is nothing wrong with talking with the preacher after services, but if a guest approaches, let the preacher speak to the guest then return to you.

Many of these things are simple ideas that we know are important to us when we visit elsewhere. Let's realize they are important to our guests also and do our best to make them feel welcome. "Therefore, whatever you want men to do to you, do also to them, for this is the Law and the Prophets" (Matthew 7:12).

—Roger Hillis

Friends Don't Let Friends Go to Hell

Everyone is surely aware of the national advertising campaign on television and radio that encourages the use of a "designated driver" and even advocates taking car keys away from a drunk person so that he won't get behind the wheel. It features the catchy phrase – "Friends don't let friends drive drunk."

As a spin-off of that idea, you've probably also seen the bumper stickers that say, Friends don't let friends drive Fords (or Chevys or Toyotas or whatever). Unless you work at one of those companies, you likely smile when you see one of those bumper stickers.

One phrase is serious; one is intended to be humorous. Here's an even more serious thought. A true friend would not even consider letting a close friend go to hell for eternity. Or would he?

Do you have friends, relatives, neighbors, co-workers, or fellow students that you have never talked to about their souls? These are people who will be lost if they don't learn about Jesus and obey the gospel. You might be the only New Testament Christian with an opportunity to say something that could change their eternal destiny. Why haven't you said something to them?

I realize that fear is a natural factor and that many of us are afraid of doing something that would make a friend mad at us. We like to avoid conflict and don't want to hurt another person's feelings.

But what is more important, staying comfortable and allowing your friend to go to hell forever, or taking a chance and maybe seeing your friend eternally in heaven? Which option would be more important to a true friend? Which would God have you to do?

I know this isn't easy for most of us. But isn't it important enough to make it an urgent priority? Courage is not the absence of fear, but the determination to do what is right despite our fear.

Be a true friend to the lost people in your life. Friends don't let friends go to hell.

—Roger Hillis

Strengthening the Local Church

Self-Evaluation Survey

Answer those questions that apply to you and your life.

1. How would you rate yourself spiritually, on a scale of 1 to 10 (with 10 as highest)?

2. Attendance (Hebrews 10:25)
   - Do you miss services when you could come?
   - Do you put other things first on a regular basis (Matthew 6:33)?
   - Do you attend Sunday morning Bible study? If not, why not?

3. Giving (2 Corinthians 9:6-7)
   - Do you give sacrificially?
   - Do you think you contribute your fair share to the Lord's work at this church?
   - Do you consider yourself to be materialistic (where on a scale of 1 to 10, with 1, not at all, and 10 being completely so)?

4. Personal Bible Study (Romans 10:17)
   - Do you study the Bible regularly (most days, if not daily)?
   - Do you study merely to prepare for class, or do you also study for your own personal growth and development?

5. Nurturing your children (Ephesians 6:4)
   - Do you help your children prepare their Bible class lessons?
   - Do you work with your children to help them apply the classes, sermons, etc. to their lives?
   - Do you bring the Bible into personal situations, like accepting defeat, getting along with other children, obeying your requests, etc.?
   - Do you have any questions about specific problems with your children that the elders could help you with?
   - If you do not have children of your own, do you try to help encourage the children of others spiritually?

6. Prayer (1 Thessalonians 5:17-18)
   - How would you rate your prayer life (again, 1 to 10)?
   - Do you pray regularly with your spouse about your relationship and other things?

7. Using talents (Matthew 25:14-30)
   - Are you helping by teaching classes?
   - Are you currently working with someone to convert them to Christ? If so, do you pray about it regularly?
   - Is the man of the house working to prepare himself to serve as an elder or deacon? If so, what qualifications do you currently lack?
   - What areas of your life should you work on so you can serve in this way?
   - Are the other members of the family trying to qualify themselves to be the child/spouse/etc. of an elder or deacon?

8. What kind of influence are you at work, school, etc.?

9. Do you help with visitation of the sick, shut-ins, etc.?

10. How do you feel about the goals, congregational direction, etc.? Is there anything about the church (positive or negative) that you would like to discuss with the leaders?

— Roger Hillis

www.ingramcontent.com/pod-product-compliance
Lightning Source LLC
LaVergne TN
LVHW020930090426
835512LV00020B/3293